EXiting the **JW** Cult:
A Healing Handbook

EXiting the **JW** Cult: A Healing Handbook

FOR CURRENT & FORMER JEHOVAH'S WITNESSES

Bonnie Zieman

Dedication

Dedicated to all who know they are meant to live in freedom & truth

Disclaimer: This book is intended as a reference volume only, and not as a medical or psychological manual. The information given here is designed to help the reader make informed decisions about recovery from membership in a cult and the consequences of leaving a cult. It is not intended as a substitute for any treatment that may have been prescribed for you by your doctor. If you suspect you have a medical or psychological problem, get help from a competent medical health professional. Do not delay seeking medical help, disregard medical advice, or discontinue medical treatment because of information in a book, including this one. Reliance on any information or suggestions in this book or recommended resources is undertaken solely at your own risk.

Contents

Acknowledgments

*T*his book could not have been written without the unwavering love, support, encouragement and always cogent feedback of my husband, Terry. I also owe a huge debt of gratitude to Vanessa for her editing, Taira for her valuable feedback, and Jordan for his technical support.

CHAPTER 1

Introduction

This book has been a long time in the making. The irony is it could not have been written had I not spent thirty years of my life as a disinclined, unfulfilled Jehovah's Witness. As a teenager and young adult I tried to imagine ways I could quietly disentangle myself from the web the JW cult weaves around one. My immediate family circumstances were such that I did not feel able to make a clean break and just walk away. It seemed my exiting process would require a rather slow, prolonged fade. There is no one way, no right or wrong way to leave this cult. There are simply individual ways of exiting that unfold as they will. I will share some of the story of my exit out of the Jehovah's Witness organization in the next few pages.

After I did make my way out, I began to formally study psychology as a student in a couple of different schools of psychotherapy. Part of my motivation for so doing was an attempt to better understand what I had been through as a member of Jehovah's Witnesses. I also wanted to learn how to manage all the painful emotions that result from spiritual abuse and reconnect with basic needs that went unmet while in the cult. Of course I hoped to develop a new vision for my life - one that was sound, reality-based and above all, finally mine.

A few years doing my own personal therapy helped heal the wounds suffered from being a member of this controlling cult, revisit missing steps in my own development due to the limited life allowed in the cult, and untie some of the knots (nots!) in the constricted JW approach to life that tagged along with me even once I had exited. Poet, Jean Toomer says: *"We learn the rope of life by untying its knots.*" Once I became a licensed psychotherapist I spent two decades helping people untie the unwanted knots of their life and I want to bring that same expertise and experience to help anyone who has suffered from being a member of the JW cult. Together in this healing handbook for current and former JWs, we will unravel some of the knots that keep one tied to the cult and that can constrict and choke a life even once out of it.

This healing handbook has information and approaches for anyone trying to find freedom and dignity as a fully-functioning, independent adult. No matter what our background, what our cultural origins, what our position, what our present beliefs, we are each called by life to develop into an authentic, autonomous, responsible adult. The roads we take to achieve autonomy and authenticity are different. Whatever the path there are some tried and true ways of walking it that will make the journey easier, more fulfilling and more meaningful. I will share a few that I know of with you here.

We will look at how to cope with the process of change, the inevitability of loss, ways to bear our losses, how to re-educate ourselves in preparation for a new life, and we will look at practical strategies designed to help with recovery from undue influence, betrayal, abuse and profound disappointment. Wherever you are in your current relationship to the Jehovah's Witnesses, you will find valuable information here to help you feel more prepared and more able to move on to enjoy a free, fulfilling life.

Actual *doctrines* of the Jehovah's Witnesses will be discussed only where they have a bearing on a person's relationship with the cult or, even more importantly, with themselves. There are already many excellent resources exposing the deceptions and flaws in the dogma of the JW cult. The destructive *practices* of the cult's governing body will be discussed here and there throughout the book especially with regard to the lingering effects they have on human lives. This book is designed to help you recover from what is an unavoidably complex relationship with this repressive organization. It is not specifically designed to awaken anyone from the trance of being one of Jehovah's Witnesses, although I would never be opposed to it serving that purpose.

If you are reading this book it is a good indication that you are awakening or already AWAKE! (Love using that word, in that way!) So much great work is already being done by many well-informed ex-JW activists. If you are still looking for evidence that JW doctrines, policies and procedures are unfounded, and violations of basic human rights check out credible ex-JW internet sites and read the books of former JW governing body member, Raymond Franz: "*Crisis of Conscience*" and "*In Search of Christian Freedom*". Though such websites and Franz's books are anathema for JWs, do find the courage to disregard the governing body's efforts to control your intake of information. Ray Franz was a man of integrity and you will be impressed by the balanced account of his journey both in and out of the Watchtower organization.

The focus of this book is more on the *process* of being a Jehovah's Witness, leaving the cult - the disruptions, the knots, the repercussions, the wounds, and the ways personal development is impeded by it - rather than on the *content* of what we were required to believe as Witnesses. Above all, ways to heal from the many painful consequences of being a JW and ways to deal with the serious repercussions resulting from the courageous act of daring to leave the cult will be shared here.

CHAPTER 2

Member of Anointed Provides a Final Push – Out

After thirty long years as one of Jehovah's Witnesses I had finally had enough. For many years I had wanted to leave the cult but was intimidated by the their threat of destruction at God's Battle of Armageddon and even more daunted by their threatened punishment of permanent estrangement from my JW family of origin. A fierce struggle between the value of family and the value of freedom raged within. It was a terrible double bind. Whichever choice I made, something precious would be lost. As a current or former Jehovah's Witness you too must be familiar with this excruciating, catch-22 impasse. But somewhere inside I knew, as religious philosopher Hildegard Von Bingen, wrote way back in the twelfth century, *"We cannot live in a world that is not our own, in a world that is interpreted for us by others. An interpreted world is not a home. Part of the terror is to take back our own listening, to use our own voice, to see our own light."*

Over a period of several years I had been trying to slowly back away from the JW organization, take back my own voice, my own listening and my own light. As author Elizabeth Gilbert, in "Eat, Pray Love" says: *"The only thing more unthinkable than leaving was staying; the only thing more impossible than staying was leaving. I didn't want to destroy anything or anybody. I just wanted to slip quietly out the back door, without causing any fuss or consequences, and then not stop running until I reached Greenland."*

To eventually *"slip quietly out the back door"* of this cult and escape to my own *"Greenland"* I had begun to skip meetings and was rarely presenting myself to go in the door-to-door ministry. My husband, an elder, was being counseled by the other elders in the congregation to get his unsubmissive wife under control, to get her to the meetings and back in the service. When that didn't work they must have hoped some admonition from a member of the "anointed class" would persuade me to change my errant, inactive ways.

Sister "Anointed", a member of the remnant of the 144,000 anointed came to our door. I invited her in expecting to hear some hollow but polite encouragement. The encouraging part of what she had to say was brief. It did not take long until she began to try to chastise and shame me:

Sister "Anointed": ... *It's obvious that you have succumbed to the temptations of the world, Bonnie. Materialism has become your stumbling block. You are opting for the good life and taking the easy way out.*

Me: *You imagine I'm not coming to meetings because I'm materialistic? Materialism is not the problem. The "isms" that could be stumbling blocks for me are more likely to be fundamentalism, dogmatism and elitism.*

Sister "Anointed": *Well, I don't know about all your fancy words, I just know **you** are taking the easy way out. It's hard to be in the truth and its obvious to me that Bonnie Zieman wants all the things a worldly life would offer.*

Me: *I agree it's hard to be in the truth. It's hard to live with all the requirements and expectations. But it is twice as hard to ever think of leaving! The Society makes sure there is no easy way to leave. If someone leaves anyway, the Society punishes them by cutting them off from all their friends and family. You think that is easy?! I imagine that leaving requires tremendous courage! **You**, Sister "Anointed", **you** want to believe that my missing meetings and service is because I am materialistic and thereby diminish the significance of how I live my life and how I raise my children.*

Sister "Anointed": *I'm not here to talk about me, I'm here to tell you that you need to think very carefully about being seduced away from the truth into an easy life in Satan's system of things.*

Me: *If I ever left, it would mean I would lose everything I have ever believed in and known. I would lose the companionship of my family. Why* *every member of my family is a Jehovah's Witness! If I left, my mother would not understand and it would break her heart! You think that would be easy?*

Sister "Anointed": *It looks like you are willing to sacrifice a lot of very important things, so that you can enjoy a life of worldly treasures and ease. But believe me it won't be easy when you have to watch your children die at Armageddon!*

Me (after taking a deep breath): *Now it's exactly that kind of not-so-subtle threat that raises all kinds of alarms for me about this organization. I think it's best if you leave now.*

It is clear Sister "Anointed" could never understand my position. But ultimately it didn't matter to me whether she understood or not. My life had been difficult in the 'religion' and it had been twice as difficult trying to find a way to honorably leave it. Once I was able to totally extricate myself it would still be difficult for a long while. But that is the price one pays to live free and dear Sister "Anointed" played an important role in convincing me that I should pay it. Meister Eckhart says, *"And suddenly you know: It's time to start something new and trust the magic of beginnings."* I knew. I could no longer just inch my way out. It was time to trust that I could survive leaving and begin a new life outside of the organization.

(Sister "Anointed" is the mother of "JW Anna" who plays a prominent role in one chapter of my memoir *"Fading Out of the JW Cult: A Memoir"*. They were both, it seems, intent on interfering in my life.)

That uncomfortable conversation of years ago illustrates just how challenging it is to try and extricate yourself from the Jehovah's Witness organization. In spite of that sister's 'loving encouragement' to remain a part of the flock, I began to work even harder to make my way out. While knowing I had to walk away, when I finally did, it actually felt like I ended up crawling out - wounded - and I had. It seemed I was only able to limp at first into my new life. It is my hope that with this book I can offer you a hand up so that you can walk tall, proud and steady into your new life of freedom.

CHAPTER 3

Leaving the JW Cult & Getting an Education

I was born into a family of Jehovah's Witnesses and eventually married into another long-standing family of Witnesses. Grandparents on both sides of my family were JWs. Right after high school I started pioneering (full-time ministry for Jehovah's Witnesses) and became a special pioneer when I married my special pioneer, elder husband. My husband was the presiding overseer (the title used then) of a French-speaking congregation. We served where the need was great in Quebec, Canada. During thirty years in the cult I was a reluctant Witness although I hid my doubts and disinclinations as one would have to, in order to be a special pioneer. My struggle was a silent, inner one.

My childhood family life was less than ideal as my father was frequently absent and often did not provide for the family during his absences. Eventually he totally disappeared from our lives (partly because of pressures from the Watchtower Society) never to be heard from again. I'm now aware that family instability and my mother using what she though was a religion to compensate for her loneliness once my father disappeared, complicated my relationship with the Jehovah's Witness organization and my ability to leave it.

I took this photograph of my little sister and my mother in front of the Kingdom Hall on Burnhamthorpe Road in the west end of Toronto. The meeting schedule is posted on the door. I spent my teenage years going in and out of those wooden doors for meetings and pre-service meetings.

I was devoted to my mother, loved her wonderfully wacky sense of humour, admired her chutzpah, marvelled at her exceptional knowledge of the scriptures, and her skills in the field ministry. As I became more and more disillusioned with the 'religion' I still could not allow myself to consider leaving, disappointing her or losing contact with her. So, I realize now, I became a very inauthentic version of myself. Like many other young JWs I let everyone think that I was happy being a Jehovah's Witness. In fact I was often pointed out as an example of what a good, young Witness should be. The dichotomy between my praiseworthy behaviours and what I *really* felt about it all made me feel like a hypocrite, before myself and Jehovah. Jehovah's Witness children often experience such authenticity and identity issues.

While for so many years I did not feel able to stand up for myself and express what I really thought about the movement's teachings and activities, when I became a mother everything changed. I did not want my children's minds polluted with the toxic ideology of the cult. I wanted no part in coercing them to peddle books and magazines in the field ministry nor was I willing to lead them into believing doctrines I had long doubted and for which I had developed feelings of disdain.

Therefore, when my first daughter was about four years old I began what could be called a slow fade out of the organization. I lessened the time I spent knocking on peoples' doors, I skipped meetings and I slowly began to open my mind to other world views by reading books by people such as Joseph Campbell (*The Power of Myth*), Stephen Levine (*A Gradual Awakening*) and Marilyn Ferguson (*The Aquarian Conspiracy*). It was exciting to read fresh, new ideas instead of the stale, repetitive gobbledygook in the JW literature.

My husband was still an elder and the assembly servant for our circuit while I was flirting with inactivity. This made it difficult for both of us. He was repeatedly counseled to get his "*rebellious*" wife under control and back to the meetings. I felt bad about the undue pressure my slow fade brought upon him as an elder and did not know if our marriage would survive my ever-increasing, inactive status. Happily it did. Terry became inactive about a year or so after I did. Somehow, neither my husband nor I were ever "*disfellowshipped*" although there were some unsuccessful attempts to get us to present ourselves before their kangaroo court or as they prefer to call it - judicial committee.

As both of our JW families realized that we had not just become "*spiritually weak*" but had made deliberate decisions to leave, they slowly began to cut us off. We are now not invited to any family events such as weddings, funerals, family reunions; nor are we informed of births, accomplishments, illnesses or deaths in the family. We have been totally excluded from our loved ones' lives and activities. Our children grew up with basically no extended family - no aunts, uncles or cousins - not because they didn't have any, but because we were shunned by them. Terry and I eventually had three beautiful children and have lived happily ever after... well... mostly...We each had some serious JW exit recovery and healing work to do. Grieving and healing work can sometimes strain a relationship.

You can read much more about the details of my life as a Jehovah's Witness - episodes of my life while in the cult, while leaving it, and while recovering after leaving - in my book "*Fading Out of the JW Cult: A Memoir*". Exiting the JW cult was one of the hardest things I have ever done, and one of the very best. I have never regretted it.

Leaving and adjusting to being out of the organization was not easy, however. There were no such things as social media networks when I left. There were few books that affirmed my instincts about the cult and if there was any material out there by other people who had already made their escape I did not come across it. There was only one book I knew of, written by an actual "apostate" and that was, "*Thirty Years a Watchtower Slave*" by William Schnell. Having seen my mother staunchly refuse to accept it as a gift from a householder while we were out together in the ministry I still, even as an ex-JW, could not bring myself to read it. So I had no outside input at that time to help confirm my decision to leave.

I now know that governing body member, Raymond Franz left the organization about the same time I did but I had no knowledge of the upheaval at Brooklyn Bethel at that time, and did not discover Ray Franz's books until many years later. It would have been nice to have known that others felt they had no choice but to leave too, and why.

My mother and sister who remained loyal Jehovah's Witnesses did not totally shun myself and my family at first, but the relationship began to change to one of friendly but only occasional and necessary communication. It hurt to feel set aside by them. If and when we did spend a few hours together they expressed no interest in my activities, never ever asking a question about my life (interests, university studies, professional life, friends, etc.). It was implicitly communicated that they wanted to know nothing about my so-called "*worldly*" life. I always wondered if they were afraid to know anything in case they too, might be tempted to leave. I spent a couple of years feeling lonely, sad, depressed, somewhat guilty and had no idea how to cope with or manage my fluctuating emotional state. Perhaps that is one reason why I decided to study psychology at a local community college.

Those courses in psychology whet my appetite for more and I enrolled in a Gestalt Therapy training program, later switching to a three year program in Psychosynthesis Psychotherapy (developed by Italian psychiatrist Roberto Assagioli, a contemporary of Freud and Jung) in order to train to become a psychotherapist.

During those intensive training programs students were required to do their own course of therapy. In that therapy I was able to piece together the pieces of my JW story, feel understood, express my pain and anger, and finally get on the road to healing from what I learned were mind-control, spiritual abuse and abandonment issues.

Once trained in two different schools of therapy, university beckoned. Of course, like all Jehovah's Witnesses, I had been discouraged from pursuing any kind of higher education. Now free to make my own choices I applied to a large university, was accepted as a 'mature' student, and majored in a program called *Applied Social Science*" (a program for people wanting to become social workers, therapists or community activists/leaders.)

Further along I obtained a graduate diploma in the teaching and training of adults. Then the areas of psychology and education were merged when I obtained a Master's Degree in Education (M.Ed.) by doing a thesis on applying a model of experiential learning (Kolb) to clinical supervisions of student psychotherapists. A few years later I was accepted into a program to obtain a doctorate (Ph.D.), but then a beautiful little grand daughter was born and we had just moved to a large property outside of the city that required a lot of maintenance, so I withdrew from the doctoral program to enjoy more important things. You do not have to be in a formal educational setting to continue learning. I marvel at all I would have missed had I remained a dutiful servant in that strict, education-phobic cult.

With the above-described formal education and training under my belt it was time to open my own office and begin private practice as a psychotherapist. I spent over twenty years working with clients, occasionally leading workshops or seminars, and supervising student therapists. It has all been very rewarding and, again, would never have been possible if I had not been willing to weather the storm of leaving the JW cult. I feel such joy that I was finally able to walk away from their so-called truth! Perhaps I should credit the cult with some of the therapeutic listening skills used every day in my work. I wonder how many thousands and thousands of hours I spent listening to their vapid, tortuous talks? Listening to clients in therapy was so much more interesting!

I share all of the above to orient you a bit in my JW history and establish the credibility required to presume to offer suggestions on how to heal the wounds resulting from the feat of surviving as a member of the Watchtower organization and the ordeal of severing connections with it.

My university studies and additional therapy training did not formally include the study of cults and/or recovery from them. If you want to read specifically about releasing yourself from cult mind-control and cult abuse, I encourage you to check out the fine books and website of counsellor, Steven Hassan. (See the Resource List at the back of this book.) Although my area of study was not cult mind-control per se, I do have the unique advantage of an up-close and personal, in-house study of the effects of being in the JW cult and have, of course, studied dozens of clinical books on how to deal with the traumatic effects of all types of abuse. As a therapist my clients were adults dealing with existential concerns, childhood abuse issues, interpersonal problems, cognitive/behavioral challenges, PTSD, and other traumatic or abusive events in their lives.

Post-graduate training in *"Psychotraumatology and Crisis Intervention for Post-Traumatic Stress"* and both levels of Certification in *Eye Movement Desensitization and Reprocessing (EMDR) Therapy* were also obtained. EMDR therapy is considered an excellent treatment for people suffering from post-trauma stress.

By the way, the word "disorder" is not always automatically tacked on the end of the phrase "Post Traumatic Stress" so as not to over-pathologize this normal reaction to traumatic events. For example, if you are suffering PTS after being in a bad car crash, it does not mean that you are necessarily dealing with a psychiatric 'disorder' or PTSD. It means you are dealing with a cluster of stress-related symptoms known as post trauma stress (e.g. anxiety, flashbacks, nightmares, hypervigilance, etc.). This is also the case for most survivors of the JW cult. Because you may suffer temporarily from PTS as a result of the pressures of being in and leaving the cult does not then mean you have the psychiatric disorder, PTSD. A consultation with a psychologist or psychiatrist could determine that for you.

The bilateral movement methodology called EMDR (bilateral eye movements, or bilateral taps during therapy to activate both sides of the brain) was used in my clinical practice to help attenuate the obsessive, negative thinking that can contribute to the symptom cluster known as PTS and for the more serious PTSD. If you would like to know more about bilateral stimulation therapy (EMDR) for post-trauma stress I encourage you to read Dr. Francine Shapiro's book "*Getting Past Your Past: Take Control of Your Life with Self-Help Techniques from EMDR Therapy*." Dr. Shapiro discovered and developed EMDR therapy.

It is my hope that the unique combination of personal past in the JW pseudo-religion, higher education and training, professional experience, interest and empathy can be employed here to provide insight into, understanding of, and help to recover from the trauma and pain a person experiences in, on the way out of, and once free of the cult.

The material presented here is not a psychological prescription nor is it a substitute for personal therapy. You must take responsibility for meeting your psychological needs and get actual professional help when indicated. Chronic severe depression, unmanageable anxiety, uncontrollable or persistent anger issues, substance abuse, etc. would be indicators that you need the help of a mental health professional. This book is offered as a psycho-educational tool to help you understand and cope with the psychological effects of being in, and getting out of a cult.

There is no one method or therapy that will relieve you of all pain (nor should we be relieved of all pain, as emotional pain serves an important psychological function – it makes us stop and pay attention to ourselves and our circumstances in order to determine what we need), but there are some simple suggestions that will help you better manage the predictable feelings of confusion and pain after a break with former beliefs, patterns and loved ones.

It is up to you to determine if the concepts, suggestions and strategies on these pages are right for you. Everyone is different. Not all who leave the Jehovah's Witnesses will have to deal with the same life challenges or emotional reactions. Some of us have other life issues that render leaving the JW cult even more complicated (e.g. disabilities, disintegrating marriages, sexual orientation, history of sexual abuse, history of mental illness, physical illness, addictions, financial problems, etc.). Take this opportunity to read, reflect upon, evaluate, and then judiciously select the suggestions you feel might work for you and your particular circumstances. Again, consider face-to-face professional help if your life or emotions are getting out of control and are too much for you to handle.

If even a few key pieces of information help in your adjustment to your hard-won freedom I will consider writing this book to have been a worthwhile endeavor. However, I am convinced you will find a great deal of value in the following pages. Much of the information in this book will help you normalize and make sense of your situation, feelings and reactions as you leave the cult and/or while adjusting to your freedom from the cult. Just knowing what to expect and that a particular reaction does not necessarily mean you are 'going off the deep end' can bring a lot of comfort and relief. If I had known all the information shared here when making my exit from the JW cult it would have made the process *so* much easier!

IMPORTANT: If you are experiencing any thoughts about suicide, act now to get help and call a suicide prevention hotline. Visit www. suicide.org and click on "International Suicide Hotlines" to find the number for your country.

CHAPTER 4

My Process of Adapting to Freedom

It is a strange rather antiseptic thing to try to describe on a few pages the experiences and feelings of several years of struggle and pain after leaving the Watchtower organization, but let me try to finish up the rest of my story so we can get to the important part of this book – the help for healing and recovery.

The first two to three years of being out of the JW cult were difficult. I was emotionally and physically exhausted from the stress, pressure and anxiety experienced while trying to fade out of the cult. This exhaustion meant there were few inner resources available to help me through the internal and external upheaval that occurred upon leaving behind the beliefs and activities that had been my norm. I was depleted. I hurt. While I would never have gone back, it was difficult adjusting to the uncertainties of being out. In a couple of the darkest moments suicidal thoughts did cross my mind but I knew I could never put my family through such a drastic event. Of course, suicide is almost invariably a misguided effort. People end their lives when what they really want is to end their pain. Even then I knew that intense psychological pain does not last forever, but suicide does.

(Again, if you are feeling suicidal, put down this book and visit **suicide.org** online, find the number for your country and dial it immediately.)

Terry and I are recently married in this photograph and special pioneering in Sherbrooke, Quebec. I had to learn French during this time, which was an additional stress on top of all our 'privileges'. It would be another ten years before I would be able to extricate myself from the Jehovah's Witness organization. This photograph was taken at a circuit assembly held in a high school (hence the cement block walls).

Right after exiting, niggling doubts about the decision to leave would sometimes creep into my mind. Why should my assessment of the Watchtower Society be correct when so many intelligent, upstanding people still believed it was the truth? Who did I think I was? If all of my family stayed happily attached to this organization, why couldn't I? Could I trust myself to make such an important decision? Did I even know how to make sound decisions? What kind of a person would make a decision they knew was bound to rupture treasured family ties?

Of course such doubts were evidence of the lingering, internalized mind-control that leaves one child-like, dependent on outside authority, and not sure they can trust their own decision-making skills. I had yet to learn to feel confident in my own inner authority. Inner authority develops with time and use. It would come ... but it took a while for me.

In spite of the remnants of JW programming still rattling around in my brain there were moments when I felt exhilarated and joyful about my hard-won freedom. Moments arose of deep inner knowing that escaping the psychological and spiritual oppression was the best and only choice to make (especially when I looked at my children). There was even some pride that I had finally found the courage to make it.

However, in the first few years after my exit I spent more time feeling confused, lonely and depressed than joyful or exhilarated. There was no one to talk to, no reading materials by others who had already negotiated leaving the 'religion'. Once my husband freed himself from the organization I was able to talk more freely with him but he still seemed to have some modicum of affection for, and a certain loyalty to the beliefs and the organization, which I could not relate to, so it was a while before I felt we could really commiserate on the subject.

The depressive feelings meant I cried a lot. One of my deepest regrets is that my children, especially the two young ones not yet in school and therefore home with me all day long, often witnessed their mother with tears streaming down her cheeks. Knowing now how self-referencing babies and toddlers are (they think they are both cause and effect of everything in their little world) it saddens me to think they may have thought they were the cause of my distress and tears. Babies and toddlers should see delight in the eyes of their parents. Though my children did most of the time, they must have been confused and upset by my frequent bouts of crying. (The distress was about missing close familial bonds with my mother and sister, not about leaving the JWs.)

When little ones see a parent in distress they can come to the erroneous conclusion that they must be the cause of the distress. Further, they may conclude that if they cannot keep their parent happy it must mean they are not 'good enough'. Imagine! It's mind-boggling to think of just how far-reaching the pernicious programming of the Watchtower organization can be – affecting even generations who had barely had any knowledge of, or exposure to, the cult!

I have since spoken with my children (as young adults) telling them of the things they may have experienced due to my angst after leaving the Witnesses and apologized to them that they really did not have the mother they should have had. They needed to know that they were always good enough (beyond good enough!) and my distress back then was in no way related to them. I also encouraged them to feel absolutely free to rant and rail about their mother in therapy if they ever felt the need! They never deserved to have a distressed, sometimes depressed mother. I am so sorry that the toxicity of the JW cult experience and its programming gnawed its way down into their precious little lives. It took a while for me to process and release the anger against the Watchtower organization for this effect on my children. I hope that the effects of trying to, and eventually exiting the cult, do not trickle down and confuse or hurt your children too.

Sometimes during that time period, when news on radio or television announced a serious earthquake or a war somewhere on the globe, my body would freeze - of its own accord. The ensuing thought was that it was surely the beginning of the "Great Tribulation" and I had just led my family out of "the truth"! The old programming and indoctrination went deep - right into the cells of my body - and seemed to kick back in with the slightest provocation. Fortunately in a few seconds my adult, reality-based brain would take over and shake off the ridiculous, unwarranted fears.

Being out did not mean parts of my psyche were not still stuck holding on to the old, doomsday beliefs programmed into me during years in the cult. In fact many beliefs, expectations and fears endemic to the cult were still internalized in my body/mind. With time and a bit of grit I no longer internally quaked at the news of an earthquake, famine, pestilence or the outbreak of a war. Eventually with time and more understanding the old, toxic programming dissolved.

There still remained in me at that time a deep fear of being disfellowshipped and then being *totally* cut off from my mother and sister. The elders would have loved to have some accusation that would result in our disfellowshipping. Having been abandoned by my father I was not sure I could endure being abandoned by my mother too. There was a lot yet to learn about the innate strength of human beings. Eventually I discovered I was much stronger than I ever knew...and let me assure you that you are too.

Because of the desire to not be disfellowshipped there was still concern about being seen doing something that was not approved of by the Watchtower organization, such as clinking glasses for a toast in a restaurant, purchasing a birthday card, purchasing Christmas ornaments, etc. I was out of the cult but, because of not wanting to lose contact with my family still vicariously under their control. I constantly monitored my behaviors and surveyed my surroundings for JW 'informants' who would report us to the elders. I was out, but not yet free.

In psychological terms this sort of 'ever-being-on-the-alert' behavior is known as hypervigilance and is often seen in people who have been subjected to high stress, trauma, or abuse. Hypervigilance is one of the symptoms of post-traumatic stress. As long as the distorted indoctrination and unreasonable expectations remain in place, we are still under a high degree of self-imposed, internal pressure and stress.

Somehow (just as any human who experiences the wrench of being separated from their family due to natural catastrophes, just as any human who has their worldview shattered by acts of inhumanity in war) with time, the fears and anxiety-driven thinking lessen and the wounds of loss of familial relationships begin to heal. Trust me on this. I have witnessed this both in my own life and in the lives of my clients. With time it will happen for you too. Jonathan Safran Foer in his book Everything Is Illuminated says *"...grief is replaced with a useful sadness. Every parent who loses a child finds a way to laugh again. The timbre begins to fade. The edge dulls. The hurt lessens. Every love is carved from loss. Mine was. Yours is. Your great-great-great-grandchildren's will be. But we learn to live in that love."*

It does take more time and a calling up of even more internal resilience to bear being cut off from children (especially minor children). The JW shunning policy is a blatant violation of basic human rights - the fundamental right to not have the integrity of our family subjected to outside interference. This kind of injustice and familial rupture elicit profound grief and you will find yourself in a period of extended mourning due to such treatment. With time you can perhaps occasionally compartmentalize your pain with regard to any separation or alienation from your children and thus find a way to cope and endure. It is my profound hope that some suggestions in this book will help you manage your grief.

If per chance you suffered any abuse at the hands of JW sexual predators your grieving process will be even more complex and take more time. If you are a survivor of both spiritual abuse and sexual abuse I recommend that you find a good therapist who can accompany you through the recovery process. If you cannot afford therapy then set aside as much time as you would spend seeing a therapist and use some of the suggestions offered in this book and in other credible self-help books to help yourself heal. (See the Resource Section at the end of this book.) You must make your healing a top-priority, concrete project in your life and not let the wounds fester forever.

Until you understand what is happening to you on a psychological and emotional level, until you know where and how to seek help, until you begin to feel better, you must simply put one foot in front of the other. You must simply fulfill the daily responsibilities that you have. You must just keeping breathing... keep moving... and one day... you will notice that you don't feel quite so bad.

I love the words of English poet, John Dryden:

> *"I am sore wounded but not slain,*
> *I will lay me down and bleed a while,*
> *and then rise up to fight again."*

Just keep rising up every day and doing what you have to do. Even though we might not know it, continuing with the little everyday necessities of life is one way that humans heal. Our body/mind/spirit is designed to heal and given time and a constructive, regular routine it usually does. It is at least, always a good place to start.

In the thirty years I have been out of the JW cult a lot has changed. When first visiting ex-JW sites on the internet I was shocked at things they were sharing about the drastic, even outrageous, changes in the Watchtower organization since I was an active member. It's really quite jaw-dropping to see the contortions of the governing body trying, and failing abysmally, to haul themselves into the twenty-first century! How isolated and out-of-touch are those self-appointed men? How do they imagine they can get away with all these wholesale, arbitrary and frankly embarrassing changes? How ignorant do they believe the rank and file membership are? Surely all of these changes trying to keep the organization somewhat viable in the eyes of the public and younger JW members, are contributing factors to the current hemorrhaging of the ranks.

If there were ever any doubts about this so-called religion being an elaborate scam, all the outlandish attempts at popularizing, rebranding and re-asserting control are proof to the contrary. It's sad for current rank and file trying to comprehend the erratic nature of "God's organization". Imagine the devastation for JW's who have had family members die obeying JW.org orders and then see those very orders adjusted, willy-nilly, by the governing body just a few years down the road!

If you have experienced hardship (or even death) in your family due to acquiescing to JW rules, or if you have had to deal with sexual abuse perpetrated by a member of the congregation and then callously mishandled by the elders, your emotional injuries and your healing process are of course compounded. As you reclaim your life, your work will be not only to heal from the spiritual and emotional abuse but also to heal from any abuse to your body's integrity and any abuse to the integrity of your family. Just as a doctor needs to treat *all* the injuries sustained in a bad accident, so too you need to address *all* the wounds sustained from your affiliation with the Jehovah's Witness cult. Then no wounds will go unacknowledged or unattended.

Healing from abuse of all kinds is being done by people across the globe. It *is* possible to recover from abuse and trauma. If you apply yourself to healing as diligently as you would to recovering from a serious surgical intervention, you too will heal.

When we cut off association with the Jehovah's Witness cult it is a symbolic surgery, isn't it? It's a courageous act of severing ties to a toxic 'religious' body. Whether literal or symbolic, major surgery requires time, attention and loving self-care to heal! Read on for valuable information that will help you better understand how to cope with emotional injuries sustained as a result of being a member of the Jehovah's Witnesses cult.

CHAPTER 5

The Positives of Exiting the JW Cult

Before we consider the challenges that will arise when we choose to exit the Watchtower organization let's remind ourselves of all the life-enhancing results we can expect once out. Of course, the obvious benefits are that we will have redefined "truth" and reclaimed our right to be free. Freedom and truth will again be ours! Here are two lists of other benefits you will also enjoy once out of the JW cult. These lists are by no means comprehensive. I'm sure you will be able to add many more positives.

We are finally free to:

1. own our life and really live
2. luxuriate in reclaimed hours, days, years
3. explore, experiment, discover
4. learn new, exciting things
5. travel the world
6. set our own agenda
7. get to know our true self
8. have fun in the manner of our choosing
9. experience joy, contentment, peace
10. revel in self-determination
11. delight in all manner of creative expression

12. cultivate a wide range of interesting friends
13. truly be a part of this big, wide world
14. ask questions and challenge perceptions
15. use our curiosity and intellect
16. get an education
17. celebrate life in a myriad of ways
18. choose and decide as we see fit
19. enjoy our sexuality as we see fit
20. have the option to sleep in on weekends

We are finally free from:

1. Watchtower's rigid, imposed schedule for our life
2. undue influence on so many of our choices
3. unrelenting, unrealistic expectations
4. constant pressure and stress
5. threats of destruction at Armageddon
6. imagined dates for the end of the world
7. having to drag ourselves out in the preaching work
8. having to study same old material over and over again
9. having to report to anyone about how we spend our time
10. all the rules about what we can read, watch or listen to
11. all the codes of dress and grooming
12. spending our vacations at their conventions
13. wondering who might be looking over our shoulder
14. being reported to the elders for some bogus misdeed
15. being expected to report others for their misdeeds
16. not being able to participate in community activities
17. not being able to participate in cultural celebrations
18. cognitive dissonance adjusting to "new truths"
19. being considered a servant, a sheep, a publisher
20. going along with whatever the governing body decides
21. having sexual police in our bedrooms
22. telling our children all the things they cannot do
23. seeing our children remain on the sidelines at school
24. having to worry about refusing blood if we need it

25. interdictions about using the internet
26. interdictions about educating ourselves or our children
27. taking menial jobs so we can better serve Jehovah
28. having to find kingdom halls when we are on vacation
29. having our children associate with protected pedophiles
30. the congregation gossip mill
31. associating with people we would never choose ourselves
32. pretending the emperors are wearing clothes
33. not knowing or expressing who we really are
34. psychosomatic ailments due to so much repression
35. having to defend how we spend our time or money

Wow! I enjoyed constructing these two lists and it must be said, they are really incomplete. You must have many more items that you could add. These lists, are however, adequate enough to affirm our instincts to leave or our already having left. What a monumental relief to be out of that oppressive cult!

Of course, that is the good news. The bad news is that in spite of all the positives we will enjoy once out, we leave somewhat brainwashed and emotionally, psychologically and spiritually wounded. If that is not enough the organization has found a way to keep hurting us even once we have made our escape.

The governing body does not take kindly to anyone who dares to point out their deceptive and injurious practices and has instituted rules about how anyone who deigns to think of defecting must be treated. They do everything within their power to keep members from leaving with any integrity and dignity. The way we are treated if we want to leave is inhumane. We are threatened, coerced, put on trial and banished from our friends and family when they get wind of our changing allegiance. We leave still struggling with the effects of their brainwashing, the wounds suffered while making our escape, and then the horrible blow of exclusion, loss of family and isolation. That is why I have written this "healing handbook". We all can use a little help to cope with and heal from their institutional abuses and continuing onslaughts.

CHAPTER 6

Thinking of... Process of... and Adjusting After... Exiting

This ex-JW healing handbook is designed to help you whether you are:

- a Jehovah's Witness who is *thinking of exiting* the cult
- a Jehovah's Witness *currently in the process of exiting*
- an ex-Jehovah's Witness *adjusting to life after exiting*

All stages of an exit from this controlling cult, masquerading as a religion, can be painful and challenging. I did not necessarily face all the challenges you may be facing or have faced, but I did finally manage to exit the cult. My exit may not have been the most accomplished or graceful, but I did exit. I have now been free of Jehovah's Witness interference and unwanted influence in my life for many years and can assure you it is possible to leave and come out happy, psychologically healthy and fulfilled on the other side.

All the indoctrination, undue influence, mind control and threats of punishment make it difficult to contemplate exiting, to think independently, to walk away and lay claim to your one and only life. Let's take a close look at some of the **challenges you can expect** to face in each stage of the exit process and some concrete **things you need to know** to support yourself through the challenges of each stage. Forewarned is forearmed, right?

Some challenges and accompanying feelings you may face *while thinking of exiting the cult*:

- **your internalized interdictions** against reading or watching any-thing that criticizes Jehovah's Witnesses. You have been warned over and over that so-called apostate materials are inspired by the devil and must be avoided at all cost. This strong prohibition can keep 'true believers' from doing the research they need to do to feel convinced they are making the right decision about their im-pulse to leave.

- **the fear and guilt** you may experience when you dare to defy the Witness interdictions and threats, and go ahead and read or watch materials that expose them. Perhaps you imagine that Jehovah is watching you. Perhaps you imagine you are vulnerable to the so-called *"mentally-diseased"* apostates and will be seduced by their reasoning. You have been programmed to believe these distorted JW exaggerations. You have the impulse to do some research to feel more confident about your decision, but you may feel some guilt about disobeying the 'faithful and discreet slave's prohibition against viewing *'worldly'* and so-called *'demonic'* information about the 'religion'.

- **the disillusionment** you will feel as you make shocking discover-ies about the Jehovah's Witness organization, their beliefs, their policies, their practices, that are not generally known by rank and file Witnesses. Expect to experience both shock and anger about what you discover.

- **the fear and powerlessness** you may experience when you con-template following through and acting based on your discoveries and misgivings about the organization. You have been groomed to not trust your own judgment, to not be independent and to rely only on the organization to reveal everything you need to know. Thus you may not feel quite up to the task of acting on your inner knowing ... yet.

- **the dread** you feel as you imagine being called before a commit-tee of elders for your change of heart, your thoughts, speech or actions. Judicial committees, disfellowshipping, marking, loss of privileges are all used as threats to keep JW rank and file from exercising their human right to think and act on their own behalf, or to change their mind.

- **the fear and dread** you feel about being disfellowshipped and then being shunned and misunderstood by family and friends. All humans need to feel they belong and the JW organization is cunning in their use of the tactic of disfellowshipping and shunning of ex-believers from their community. You are told it is to keep the congregation clean, but another reason is to reduce future defections from the organization because of fear of the very punishments current JWs see meted out on those who dare to leave.
- **concern** about the decision you will have to make about whether you will become inactive and fade away, or whether you will write a formal letter of disaffiliation from the 'religion', or whether you will publicly declare your doubts and concerns and end up formally disfellowshipped for your changing beliefs and loyalties.
- **imagining the public shame** and humiliation you may face if you follow through on the impulse to leave the group.
- **fears** about what happens after you leave, if you do. Will you be able to make it in a 'worldly' environment? What will it be like to leave all the old beliefs and daily patterns of your life? Is the freedom you will enjoy worth the price you will have to pay? (The answer is "Yes!" by the way.)
- **the urge** you may feel to tell everyone you care about, what you have discovered about the cult and its governing body.

These are some of the daunting challenges and considerations you may face, with even more daunting consequences for acting upon them, meted out by a harsh, judgmental and punitive governing body. Thus it is really important that you **do enough research** and give serious thought to what you learn before taking the big step to set yourself free. Make time to **develop a strategic plan** to prepare yourself and your loved ones if you decide to unshackle yourself from the chains of this fundamentalist movement.

A few things that might *help* you with the above stage of *thinking about exiting*:

- **know** you are not the only one who has seen all the cracks in the Jehovah's Witness organization and considered leaving. Take this opportunity to read books, blogs, websites authored by people who have already made their exit from the cult. Check out documentaries and YouTube videos where you will see and hear other people who have lived as Jehovah's Witnesses and hear about their experiences of exiting to freedom. It is always a comfort to know you are not alone and that others have navigated the path before you. There are thousands walking it with you right now.

- **know** that you do not have to obey the orders of the governing body or their representatives, the elders. You do not have to appear before them and justify or explain anything if you do not want to. You can refuse their request to present yourself before a judicial committee and be interrogated and preached to by them. It could mean that you will be disfellowshipped but you will probably be disfellowshipped anyway, even if you attend their judicial hearing.

- **know** the majority of people who leave do not return, indicating that they remain at peace with their decision to leave.

- **know** most who leave make decent lives for themselves outside of the JW organization without falling into the clutches of any "demonic forces" or turning to a life of "debauchery", as JW.ORG preposterously claims.

- **know** people in the supposedly big, bad world out there are generally just as good and just as kind as Jehovah's Witnesses. The ubiquitous 'badness' of the world is another of the many deceptions of JW.ORG. The governing body wants you to be afraid of people in the world so that you will remain in the tight bubble of the organization. I am reminded of the words of Christopher Hitchens, "*Human decency is not derived from religion. It precedes it.*" Most Jehovah's Witness converts were good people before they converted. It is not being a Jehovah's Witness that makes people good. There are so many decent, loving, kind human beings in the world. Don't worry that you are moving away from good people (whose goodness toward you actually seems to be conditional on you remaining a JW) and won't find good people with whom to associate in the 'world'. You will! Humans are wired to be decent unless some terrible trauma or neglect interferes with their innate human decency.

- **know** that although you have been indoctrinated to believe it is a sin to leave "the truth" and that by leaving you condemn yourself to death at the Battle of Armageddon, it is just not true. You may have noticed that their Armageddon keeps being delayed. I left around 1980 and have not yet been destroyed! You have been bombarded with these threatening, fear-inducing, false ideas. You are not committing a sin to change your mind. The human mind was made to explore, discover, adapt and change. You will not die because you change your mind. You will be subject to the normal vicissitudes of life just like everyone else but death due to leaving a cult is not one of them! Such ridiculous threats are another desperate attempt by the JW organization to keep members from leaving when they discover the truth about 'the truth'.

- **know** that what you are contemplating won't be easy, but it will be so worth it to reclaim your one and only life, to reclaim your right to decide what you value, what you believe, to make your own choices, choose your own friends, and to live each sweet day *free*. However, if the decision to leave means you will be cut off from minor children who still need you as a parent you may want to seriously consider simply becoming inactive until they have reached a certain level of maturity and capacity to understand what is happening in the family.

- **know**, therefore, that if you are contemplating leaving the JWs, you must proceed very carefully. Most ex-JWs will tell you it is probably better to become inactive and slowly fade out of the 'religion' than to make a public defection and end up disfellowshipped. It is challenging enough to have to reconstruct your life without having the added burden of being shunned by family and friends, which you will be if you are disfellowshipped. To keep from being ordered to present yourself before a committee of elders and excommunicated you must be very deliberate and strategic about everything you do -- even now. For example, even if it would give you tremendous satisfaction and even if you feel sure that other JWs would want to know what you've discovered about the organization, you should seriously consider keeping what you are learning to yourself for now (unless absolutely sure you can trust the person to keep your confidence). Keep your long-term well-being in mind (and the well-being of minor children) and protect yourself from being reported to the elders. Ask yourself if it is worth the immediate gratification of exposing the JW cult in your milieu now, if it means you will be shunned by those you love in the future. I know this all sounds a bit strange, but truth be told every JW is expected to be an informant and report on anyone who seems to be thinking or acting for themselves against the edicts of the governing body. No, I am not paranoid. In fact there is a truly bizarre example of spying on myself and my family and reporting the information to the elders by a JW whom I thought was my friend, in my book, "*Fading Out of the Jehovah's Witness Cult: A Memoir*". It is wise to be cautious, judicious and strategic ... as you take steps to leave this cult.

- **know** that reading this book can help you.
- **contemplate** the powerful question of contemporary poet, Mary Oliver: "*...Tell me, what is it you plan to do with your one wild and precious life?*"

("The Summer Day", New and Selected Poems, 1992)

If you have the chance, do read another of Mary Oliver's poems, "*Wild Geese*" (Dream Work, 1994). It makes me shiver with its beautiful reminders of our basic human right to be, our basic human right to belong, and our basic human right to love what we love.

—⊷—

Some challenges and accompanying feelings you may face while actually *in the process of exiting the cult*:

- **fear of the unknown**. How exactly will everything unfold? Will I be able to fade out of the organization or will I be called on the carpet by a committee of elders and asked to justify my behaviors and beliefs? Will I have the courage to refuse the elder's orders? Will my family obey or defy the expectation to shun me?
- **doubts** about your ability to follow through with your intent to leave. Will I have the strength? Will I be able to explain what it is I am doing and why? Do I have to, or want to explain myself to a committee of elders? Can I endure the exposure and condemnation by those who don't understand my choice and aren't willing to think beyond what they have been told?
- **patience** while well-meaning Witnesses try to counsel or shame you out of your inner knowing and your intent to leave, like Sister "Anointed" in the above example.
- **anger** and perhaps bitterness at the way you are being treated by the elders and even the brothers and sisters. Discovering that the love from the friends 'in the truth' is conditional will be hurtful. When you don't follow the rules of the organization, you are cast out by people you thought loved you. There is also no acknowledgment or gratitude for all your years of service. And now that you see the truth about 'the truth' none of your previous service for the organization counts for anything if you choose to leave. There will certainly be no going-away party to thank you for your many years of service!
- **humiliation** you may feel if your situation is exposed publicly from the platform by the elders.
- **family disharmony**, turmoil and pain if your marriage mate does not see things as you do and if minor children are involved.
- **concerns** about what your minor children will be told about you and how they will feel about you as a consequence. Concerns about whether your children will remain under the control and influence of the JW cult.

These, too, are a few of the daunting challenges you can anticipate while in the process of leaving, but hopefully ones you will come to terms with as you seriously consider your options.

A few things to *help* you with *the above stage of being in the process of exiting*:

- **know** it may help you to document all the details of the process of leaving the Jehovah's Witnesses. It could prove useful down the road to have carefully documented what happened in discussions with elders, etc. As well, documentation could also serve as a way to release some of the pent-up pressure you are feeling. Set apart a few pages in a special journal to make a running list of all the reasons you have for making your decision to leave. You can go back and review this list whenever you feel your morale, memory or determination flagging.
- **know** it helps to keep reading well-documented material such as Raymond Franz's book, "*Crisis of Conscience*". Join groups or forums of ex-witnesses online where you can express yourself and hear other points of view. Keep watching YouTube videos of documentaries (such as "Truth Be Told") or of other ex-witnesses who are sharing their exit experience. (Be selective with materials on the web. While most material by ex-Jehovah's Witnesses is well-intentioned, as in anything, there are varying degrees of quality in what is available. Find sites that treat the subject seriously and ones that are suited to you.)
- **know** that it is normal for the imbedded indoctrination to still make you feel fearful of hearing the opinions, experiences and research done by people who have already left the organization. You have been programmed to believe that these ex-JW 'pagans', 'heathens', or those who proudly call themselves 'apostates' are influenced by the Devil. Did you know the Greek origins of the word *apostate* simply mean to '*stand off*' or '*stand away from*'? Did you know the Latin origins of the word *pagan* simply mean '*rural*' or '*peasant*'? The word *heathen* comes from old English word '*heath*' which refers to '*uncultivated land*'. Yet, Jehovah's Witnesses have loaded these simple, non-threatening words (used originally to describe people who lived in rural regions and thus too far away to frequent the churches in cities) with deceptive, frightening implications, so that just to hear the

words makes a Jehovah's Witness experience tremors of fear and distrust. Please be assured that while the JW programming produces powerful feelings in you, they are feelings orchestrated by a self-serving governing body and are baseless. The misinformation and fear-mongering are designed to keep you under their control. It is not dangerous to do research, to learn, to know for yourself. So-called apostates and pagans are simply human beings who hold different values and views than the JW organization. They are not evil or demonic. They do not represent a threat to you. It is your basic human right to gather information from a variety of sources. Do not allow the JW organization to deny you the right to be informed. Their archaic tactics fly in the face of rational thinking and basic human rights.

- **know** that you must take care of yourself physically during this time of decision-making and leave-taking. Make sure you are eating well, exercising, keeping yourself well-hydrated and getting enough sleep. Being physically strong will help you feel psychologically strong and, thereby, help you make better decisions on your own behalf.

- **know** that it can be helpful to find a therapist with whom you can talk about this life crisis, your reactions to it and the implications for a marriage or minor children. Consider couples therapy if your partner feels that your leaving the group is a deal-breaker for the marriage. If money is a consideration, you can try to find a university, university hospital, or a psychotherapy training center where student therapists, about to graduate, are beginning to see clients. Because they are still students and need to practice their new skills with actual clients, they sometimes offer their services at reduced rates or even on a sliding scale based on your ability to pay. While they may not be versed in 'cult exit techniques', they will provide a non-judgmental ear and some tried-and-true ways to help you manage anxiety. If seeing a therapist is not an option for you at this time, you will find help in *this* book that can provide *some* (not all) of the same benefits as a professional consultation. Some books can serve as what is known as "bibliotherapy".

The following poem can be a source of strength and inspiration as you make your way out of the JW cult:

Invictus

Out of the night that covers me,
Black as the pit from pole to pole,
I thank whatever gods may be
For my unconquerable soul.

In the fell clutch of circumstance
I have not winced nor cried aloud.
Under the bludgeonings of chance
My head is bloody, but unbowed.

Beyond this place of wrath and tears
Looms but the Horror of the shade,
And yet the menace of the years
Finds and shall find me unafraid.

It matters not how strait the gate,
How charged with punishments the scroll,
I am the master of my fate,
I am the captain of my soul.

William Ernest Henley

—⊗⊗⊗—

Some challenges and accompanying feelings you may experience *after having exited the JW cult*:

- the pain of the unjust shunning by your loved ones
- pain and anger about being judged, 'marked' and demeaned
- familial complications due to your different status with the organization
- some despair or depression due to so many losses

- anger due to all the things you sacrificed as a member of the JW cult
- confusion about how to rebuild your life
- confusion around all the decisions you will have to make during this life transition
- a pressing desire to understand what has happened to you
- wanting to remove all the old indoctrination from your mind
- contemplating whether to embrace another religion or belief system
- occasional doubts that you have made the right decision
- occasional moments of delight and joy as you revel in your hard-won freedom (this is, of course, not a challenge but I just had to remind you of it again!)

These may be some of the challenges that will come after exiting the cult but ones that will abate with time as you come to understand the import and immensity of what you have accomplished, rid yourself of all the specious indoctrination, and assign the whole experience its proper place in your life. What can *help* you with the stage of actually having left? This book! Do read on.

"Challenges in life can either enrich you or poison you. You are the one who decides."
~Steve Maraboli

"Change and growth take place when a person has risked himself and dares to become involved with experimenting with his own life."
~Herbert Otto

"The earth is all before me. With a heart Joyous, nor scared at its own liberty, I look about; and should the chosen guide Be nothing better than a wandering cloud, I cannot miss my way. I breathe again!"
~William Wordsworth

CHAPTER 7

Ways to Support Your Recovery & Healing

There is a lot of valuable information and there are many practical techniques that can accelerate and support the natural healing process after any difficult event, be it an experience that is a small 't' trauma, or a more serious experience that is a big 'T' Trauma. In broad terms (we will get to specifics in a bit) some ways I have discovered to help along the healing process after major trauma are:

- slowly *piece together a more complete understanding* of the experience that has left you distressed.
- allow yourself to *experience the feelings that arise* (grief, fear, anger, guilt, bitterness, etc.) about the experience without going into denial, pushing them away, or judging them.
- work to *accept any reactions* you have, based on what you experienced. Read materials and visit websites that can normalize your reactions to contemplating leaving, actually leaving, and then suffering punishments prescribed by the JW cult for the leaving. Everything will feel much more manageable if you have assured yourself that what you are experiencing falls within the range of what everyone else who exits also experiences.
- *educate yourself* about how to live free without an external, parental substitute determining what you are allowed to do and what you are not. Read. Study. Learn.

- *learn some basic coping skills* to help you manage the anxiety, anger, hurt, loneliness and sadness. (e.g. with the help of personal therapy, group therapy, self-help books, etc. See the suggested reading list at the back of this book.)
- *re-visit how to think critically* and how to not be stuck in a black/white, either/or view of the world. (*Think Smarter*, Michael Kallet, 2014) This will give you an expanded view of your options and help you make healthy choices for yourself. Reclaim your right to ask questions and your right to say "*No*" without guilt and without having to justify your reasons for saying "*No*". You no longer have to simply accept all arbitrary, executive orders from on high without question. You have the right to ask:

"How exactly do you know that?"
"Can you show me the research that supports what you are saying?"
"Are there alternative possibilities to consider before arriving at a decision?"

Reconnecting With Self, Needs, Values, and Goals:

- *honor your needs and desires* by taking time to determine exactly what they are for you now that you are out of the cult. When I had been out for a year or so someone asked me, in a particular situation, what I needed. I watched myself try to find what I needed and not be able to find anything at all. I realized that as a Jehovah's Witness I had been programmed to be totally disconnected from my personal wants and needs. I literally could not access a personal need! Part of my work then (and probably yours now) is to give yourself permission to have wants and needs, to reconnect with them, and honor them.
- learn how to, and practice *taking concrete steps to meet your specific needs, wants, desires* - thereby affirming who you are now apart from the Jehovah's Witness organization and their indoctrination.
- begin to *peel back the layers of the false self* you had to construct to survive in the cult. Underneath all the layers of defense (which were

appropriate then to protect yourself) is your true, authentic self waiting to be revealed. Just know you don't have to go anywhere to find or build a true self. Your true self lies within, waiting for you to strip away the false (unquestioning, acquiescent, numbed) self you had to construct to survive in the controlling, doomsday cult.

- take the time to proactively *determine what you are willing to expend your life energies on now* that you have freed yourself from the Watchtower's ever-present, demanding agenda. Reclaim the right to determine how you will spend your time and energy.

- decide to *construct a new vision of life for yourself* - one that is yours alone - not one prescribed for you by family or the Watchtower Society.

- integrate (successfully include) the part of your life dominated by the JW cult into an authentic, *meaningful understanding of your entire life experience.* (We are usually only able to do this near the end of our recovery process.)

- and eventually, when you are ready, *learn how to accept, forgive and let go* of any bitterness toward *others* that still remains (this takes time – especially forgiveness - and should definitely not be rushed or forced). Artist and writer, C.R. Strahan says, *"Forgiveness has nothing to do with absolving a criminal of his crime. It has everything to do with relieving oneself of the burden of being a victim – letting go of the pain and transforming oneself from victim to survivor."*

- *learn how to love, be kind to yourself and to forgive yourself.* Self-acceptance is the foundation for true freedom. Perhaps you notice self-recriminating thoughts about things you did as a Jehovah's Witness, like helping in the indoctrination of your Bible studies or your children, or like not finding the where-with-all to get out sooner, etc. Such recriminations and resentments against yourself are part of the toxic legacy from the cult. Refuse to allow them to continue to infect you. You do this by consciously working on self-acceptance and self-forgiveness. These two gestures are balm to the abused soul.

"I am content to follow to its source
Every event in action or in thought;
Measure the lot; forgive myself the lot!
When such as I cast out remorse
So great a sweetness flows into the breast
We must laugh and we must sing,
We are blest by everything,
Everything we look upon is blest."
William Butler Yeats
(A Dialogue of Self and Soul, Selected Poems, p. 125)

The words of American poet and Pulitzer Prize Winner for Poetry, Galway Kinnell in his poem *"Saint Francis and the Sow"* (Three Books, 2002) are especially tender and healing:

".... sometimes it is necessary
to reteach a thing its loveliness...
and retell it in words and in touch
it is lovely
until it flowers again from within,
of self-blessing; ...."
Galway Kinnell

May you too find ways to *"flower again from within of self-blessing"*.

CHAPTER 8

Moving Through
Stages of Change

Albert Einstein said, "*The measure of intelligence is the ability to change.*" Well, having left or wanting to leave JW.ORG means you are preparing to embrace many changes and must, therefore, be very intelligent! Let's look a bit at how humans are affected by significant changes. It's important to understand that a transition from being one of Jehovah's Witnesses to being an ex-JW is *a process* that moves through some fairly predictable (and sometimes challenging) stages. Knowing what to expect is half the battle.

There are many theories that have been developed to help explain and demystify the process of change. These theories outline predictable patterns and emotions one can expect to experience when going through any major transition in life. (Each journey through this change from JW to Ex-JW will be unique and your individual process may vary a bit from what you find described below.)

Typical of **the first stage** of any major change is a period of **disorientation**. You may feel disconnected, off-balance, unsteady. This is normal. To adjust you need to allow *time* and you need to seek *information* that will help you understand your experience and recalibrate yourself to your new reality. (That is what you are doing right now!) Support yourself through this period of disorientation. Take good care of yourself during this stage. It can be helpful to write down on small cards why you made this change and how you know you will benefit from the change. Keep these cards where they are easily accessed (wallet, purse, pocket, desk drawer, etc.) and refer to them often. Sometimes during this phase of disorientation you may have trouble recalling why you even made the choice you did! Don't worry you will not remain in the stage of disorientation forever!

As **the second stage** of change emerges (and the disorientation lessens) so do some **personal reactions**. You may experience feelings of fear, anger, sadness and resentment. It is important to support yourself through any strong emotions that arise. Make sure you are well nourished, well-hydrated, getting enough sleep (even extra sleep for a while) and getting adequate exercise. Bilateral movements of the body such as walking or jogging actually support the psychological re-processing of trauma in your brain (similar to EMDR therapy). If you can afford the luxury of going for therapy and can find a therapist trained in EMDR, it can be a great source of support during the stage of personal reactions. Further on in this book are many specific suggestions to help you manage emotional reactions.

Typical of **the third stage** of change is a level of **resolution, acceptance and adaptation** to the new reality. You begin to recognize and experience the benefits of the change you have made. You will feel more able to test and explore the wide range of possibilities now open to you. Be prepared for the pattern of two steps forward, one step back. You are asking your mind and body to synchronize in their adaptations to the change you have made and all of your 'parts' cannot always be in perfect sync. Know that the path to the goal is not always perfectly straight and try to just relax into the process. You're almost there!

Typically in **the fourth stage** of the change process, you feel able to **embrace the new reality** - so much so that the new reality begins to feel like second nature to you. You have incorporated the changes and their results into your everyday life. You begin to enjoy the positive effects of the big decision you made and perhaps find yourself celebrating the changes made. Woo-hoo! You're free!

It is vital to remember that life continually moves and changes and that change is a process. If you find yourself in a stage of change that is difficult, allow it, knowing that usually your psyche will judge when one stage is complete and move (when it judges the timing to be right) on to the next stage. You are no longer trapped in a stagnant, stifling situation where you have no hope for any personal change or individual growth. What a gift – to be able to move comfortably with the wonderful process of change!

Once having successfully negotiated the stages of change you will have grown, matured and expanded your sense of self and your sense of well-being.

> *"It may be hard for an egg to turn into a bird: it would be a jolly sight harder for it to learn to fly while remaining an egg. We are like eggs at present. And you cannot go on indefinitely being just an ordinary, decent egg. We must be hatched or go bad."* C.S. Lewis

Once 'hatched' out of the Jehovah's Witness cult we are like new, little fledglings who have just emerged out of the confinement of a brittle, dark enclosure! It takes time to adapt to the change, get our bearings, find our 'legs' and run freely across the land of life. How wonderful to step out of the constraints of that dark cell and explore the light-filled, crazy, complex, wondrous world around us!

> *"Change the changeable, accept the unchangeable, and remove yourself from the unacceptable."* Dennis Waitley

CHAPTER 9

Value of 'Debriefing'
(Telling Your Story)

D id you know that when a large business enterprise goes through a traumatic event they often hire an Employee Assistance Program (EAP) to help employees deal with the experience? For example, if a bank is robbed at gunpoint the bank will often hire an EAP company to help employees cope with the trauma of the incident. The EAP will send in psychologists trained in *critical incident debriefing*. These psychologists are professionals trained to offer emotional and psychological support after a trauma. The main goal of a critical incident debriefing is to prevent the development of any post-traumatic stress. Debriefing is not therapy. It is usually a one to three hour session (for a one-time incident) where the traumatized person gets to pour out their experience and really be heard. The act of completely expressing what happened to an attentive, understanding third party helps release and attenuate the stress.

Just as soldiers or covert operatives, after a dangerous mission, benefit from being required to relate everything that happened on the mission, so too people who are traumatized in everyday life benefit immensely from being 'debriefed' (encouraged to recount their story). Of course, covert operatives are mainly being debriefed for what they learned on their mission but a secondary, important benefit is to be debriefed about the danger encountered, the double-binds and the stress experienced. Learning groups and project groups are also sometimes debriefed to help group members reflect on the experience and integrate the learnings.

As a Jehovah's Witness we were subjected to mind control, undue influence, threats of destruction and threats of banishment from the tribe and many other disturbing experiences. This sort of on-going, relentless pressure is a form of trauma and needs to be 'debriefed' to help release the trauma and reflect upon what was learned from the experience. We leave the JW cult having learned a multitude of lessons that we would be wise to own. Benjamin Franklin said, "*Things which hurt, instruct.*" 'Debriefing', of some kind, helps one integrate the learnings from the trauma and resulting pain into our life.

Ex-JWs have experienced trauma (profound stress) in so many ways while trying to extricate themselves from the oppressive group. The trauma can be caused by having to appear before a judicial committee to justify their actions, or by being publicly denounced and banished from the congregation, or by being cut off from their family who are advised to shun them, etc. Unfortunately there is no formal critical incident debriefing for brave exiting JWs unless they can afford to go to a good therapist. However, if you cannot afford the cost of a therapist you can still find ways to recount your experience and name the resulting wounds.

To 'Debrief' Yourself

Create an online journal dedicated to your own 'debriefing' project *or* get yourself a large notebook and *start writing a narrative* about your Jehovah's Witness cult experience. In the journal you can:

- make a record of your life as a Jehovah's Witness.
- record all the details of the most traumatizing events.
- record how you were treated (welcomed, influenced, coerced, manipulated, etc.)
- journal about the details of any fear or shame. Record other emotions that still grip you.
- write about all the sacrifices you had to make.
- write about things you were pressured to do but did not want to do.
- write about the personal hurts, the insults.
- include the good experiences (there must be some)

- journal about what you learned from the entire cult experience, not the doctrines, but more about what you learned from being controlled, from suppressing your feelings, from discovering the deceptions, from being placed in double-bind, catch-22 situations, etc.

Writing about your experience, on your own, can be a valid and extremely helpful form of psychological debriefing. If you journal on your own you don't have to worry about chronological order or providing a detailed context, unless you want to. You also don't have to wonder if you are explaining it well enough for someone else (e.g. a therapist) to understand. You are doing it for you, so **do it in any form you choose.** Just do it! American writer, Pat Conroy, in his book 'My Reading Life" says, *"Writing is the only way I have to explain my own life to myself."* You could begin now to explain your life as a Jehovah's Witness to yourself with an informal, self-styled debriefing record.

Author, Christina Enevoldsen, who helps folks overcoming sexual abuse, says*: "It's common to reject or punish yourself when you've been rejected by others. When you experience disappointment from the way your family or others treat you, that's the time to take special care of yourself. What are you doing to nurture yourself?... Find a healthy way to express your pain."* Take "special care of yourself" and "express your pain" by writing about your experience in this doomsday cult. Have you ever noticed how someone who is in an accident, or in the hospital for surgery, or who has been mugged, etc., seems to need to tell the story of the incident over and over again? You'll often hear them say things like: *"And then.... and it took forever .... and I couldn't understand ... But eventually .... and I was so scared ... It was so .... And did I tell you ....."* They are not just deriving some narcissistic pleasure from talking about themselves. **Their psyche knows that by relating the incident over and over they initiate an inner healing process. They are releasing the trauma. Their brain is organizing, re-organizing, understanding and coming to terms with the experience** by telling it over and over. These folks who repeat their story several times to anyone who will listen are, without knowing it, informally 'debriefing' themselves.

When a major traumatic event happens the psyche compels us to relate it. You do not necessarily have to sit in front of a therapist to debrief. You can do it for yourself with a private (password-protected) online journal or with paper and pen. You may have already noticed the urge to do so. Don't ignore the urge. It is a nudge towards healing. It's following a natural instinct to heal.

One proviso: Since we usually have so much to relate after a trauma or during an on-going trauma, we need to be careful that we don't burden those close to us by relating our story repeatedly, ad nauseam. That would not be sensitive or fair. In a private journal we can record our story without overburdening the patience or sensitivities of anyone. Journaling is a great way to debrief, to honor our stories, to let go of some of the pain, and to initiate the healing process – if we choose. The goal is, at some point down the road, to close the journal and walk away from the painful story – free, relieved and renewed.

Julia Cameron, author of the book *"The Artist's Way"* (2002) suggests that her readers do *"morning pages"*. She says that artists can rid themselves of negativity and clutter in their head by journaling free form, non-stop for approximately thirty minutes every morning.

You dear JW or ex-JW are now an artist creating the masterpiece of your new, free life. You are designing a new future. What demands more creativity and artistry than re-constructing a life? This glorious act of self-renewal and life-design qualifies you as an artist! The 'creating-my-new-life artist' that you are, can also benefit from doing Cameron's "morning pages" to release negativity.

Here is my suggestion on **how to adapt Cameron's "morning pages" to your cult exit experience:**

If you find yourself experiencing a lot of grief and pain or harboring a lot of resentment and negativity about your life as a Jehovah's Witness, **create a second journal dedicated to expressing your feelings**. Use this second "morning pages" journal to allow the full and free expression of any negative feelings (e.g. anger, resentment, sadness) for thirty minutes every morning. You may have to get up a little earlier than usual to allow time for this. (Writing about your negative thoughts and painful feelings at the end of the day is less desirable. It could interfere with a peaceful night's sleep and adversely affect your dreams. What's more frightening than a having-to-go-in-field-service-again nightmare?!)

The deal is that once you have released your resentments and hurts in your journal, you then promise yourself not to fall back into the hurt and resentment again *that day*. Just that day. The next morning will dawn and you will grant yourself another thirty minutes of unbridled expression in your dedicated feelings journal, be it online or on paper. This is a healthy, every-day form of debriefing from the burden of negativity in whatever form it manifests.

Recording "morning pages a la Julia Cameron" allows you to accept and honor the feelings that are still in you, but limits their expression to a certain time and place every day. This frees you up for the rest of the day to enjoy and explore life - to be creative and productive without interference from burdensome, heavy, negative feelings about your years of servitude as one of Jehovah's Witnesses.

If during the day negative thoughts about your JW experience sneak in anyway, simply stop them, and say "*Not now*". Then 'remind them' you will give them another opportunity for full expression the next morning. Cameron's "morning pages" will then have been adapted by you as a sort of limited daily debriefing, a releasing of any pain, sadness, resentment, anger, bitterness onto the open, welcoming, non-judgmental screen or page.

In this free-form journaling do not concern yourself too much with appearance or style. Just write. There are no extra points for perfect prose. For thirty minutes of journaling anything goes. *Another proviso* however, is that you should stop if you see yourself getting too emotional or worked up. **The important thing is to keep it all in proportion, safe, contained in the journal, and limited to thirty minutes.** Deal? Deal!

You should have one journal for your "morning pages" expression of feelings and another separate journal where you tell the story of your JW history. The morning pages journal is a holding place for feelings, while the other journal will become the narrative of your entire experience in the cult.

It never occurred to me to journal when I first faded out of the JW organization. Why I had no idea what the word 'debriefing' even meant back then. So my backload of emotion churned away within, doing the damage that is done when one has no way to express or release the pressure of years of suppressed feelings. Many years after fading out of the cult I finally had the benefit of therapy and was able to examine the experience, begin to understand the pain, articulate my grief and release the burden of emotion carried for so many years. All the reading done during my studies further helped me to identify still festering emotions and come to terms with my JW past. I then believed that the large part of my recovery work was complete.

Now writing this handbook, I am at the same time writing a memoir of my personal experiences in and out of the JW cult. As I write and put chronological order to so many experiences related to being a JW and an ex-JW, I am amazed at links and connections made that had not been made in therapy and during years of study. Certain patterns, needs, longings, choices, personal idiosyncrasies, etc. make more sense to me because of this current writing.

All these years later, writing this book and a memoir, I am benefiting from a form of informal, self-directed, belated debriefing. My understanding of the effects of the entire JW experience falls even more clearly into place and the whole writing experience has had an unexpected, belated, therapeutic effect. I was surprised by this and share it with you to show the power of writing down your story – whenever you are able to get around to it. Now that you know you can 'debrief' yourself, don't wait. If you have to wait, my recent writing experience is proof that it can still do its work way down the road. If you decide to take up the challenge to write down your experience, you will find it to be an illuminating, satisfying, extremely therapeutic part of your recovery from cult oppression.

> *"Give sorrow words.*
> *The grief that does not speak*
> *Whispers the o'erfraught heart and bids it break."*
> Shakespeare, Macbeth

CHAPTER 10

Becoming Comfortable With Feelings

A re you a bit afraid of the feelings still rattling around in your heart and mind about your experiences in the Jehovah's Witness organization? Are you concerned that if you allow yourself to experience or express feelings or emotions, you might not be able to stop? Are you afraid they might overwhelm you and that you could get totally caught up in them? Are you trying hard not to feel your anxiety or pain? Here are a few things that are helpful to know about emotions and the expression of them:

- Although we often use the terms "emotions" and "feelings" interchangeably, they are not quite the same. Neuroscientist, Dr. Sarah McKay, explains: "*Emotions play out in the theater of the body. Feelings play out in the theater of the mind*". For the purposes of this book, however, we will not get too 'hung-up' on using each of the terms with medical precision. It is just good to begin this discussion with a proper definition of terms.
- E-motions are designed to move through you, if you allow them. An emotion, in a basically healthy person, does not emerge and get stuck on "play". Emotions are like a wave on the ocean - they rise, they fall, and then disappear, moving back into the ocean from whence they came - unless we suppress the initial appearance of the wave. Once the emotion is acknowledged or expressed, the wave of emotion may rise again later needing more expression, and then it

too will fall away back into the sea. *Allow emotions* as you can, and as appropriate, to move freely through you.

- We all experience painful feelings and emotions and our body/ mind is equipped to deal with them. Pain only turns into suffering when we resist it. Stop resisting your emotions, your pain. Psychological and emotional pain is often the precursor to growth. We are here to grow (not remain static) and pain, whether we like it or not, helps us to do that. Emotional pain is an expression of who we are and what we are experiencing at a given time. Pain often manifests in the form of different feelings (sadness, anger, resentment, fear, etc.) Honor your pain by allowing it and giving it the appropriate expression it deserves. The word 'appropriate' is important. Expression of difficult emotions is not a license to frighten or abuse anyone – including yourself. Make sure your expression of feelings happens in an appropriate place, at an appropriate time, in an appropriate way. Otherwise you are just recklessly spewing toxins of suffering all over yourself and the environment. Gary Zukav says, "*Choosing not to act on an angry impulse and to feel the pain that lies beneath it is a very courageous thing to do.*"

- Painful emotions are generally quite short-lived (during a particular expressive event) *if* we do not resist them. It is our resistance to them that prolongs them. If we shove aside an emotion it does not go away. It just buries itself in the tissues of our body/mind waiting for another moment to arise and capture our attention. If we constantly suppress our emotions the pressure for release builds inside, can be experienced as anxiety or even panic, and can interfere with the full, expression of who we are.

- As a therapist I began to notice that even people who were expressing the deepest levels of pain (crying, ranting, wailing) never went much beyond 10-15 minutes at the very most, in one emotionally expressive event. The body/mind seems to know how much pain the human organism can tolerate at a given time, and of its own accord the psyche seems to bring the feeling and its expression naturally to a close. I have witnessed this over and over again in both myself and others. Normal painful emotions will move through you (e-*motion*) and bring you relief in a relatively brief period of time, *if you honor them and allow them.* The psyche knows how to shut down (after a brief period of expression) on its own and you will then be free, with a lighter heart, to move on to the next thing on your agenda. One brief session of allowing an emotion may not complete its release, however. The same feeling may arise again at a later time asking for more expression. Honor the unique process and pace of your emotions. As a JW you had to suppress so many of your true feelings that you may have a backload waiting for expression. Your 'feelings' journal will help you with this.

- Jill Bolte Taylor, brain scientist, in her book "*My Stroke of Insight*" tells us that the natural life span of an emotion is about a minute and a half! If the emotion continues, she says, it is because it is being fed by further thoughts. If you feel stuck in an emotion or feeling, examine the thoughts running through your mind at the time. Then stop feeding the feeling with any further thoughts. It is often our thinking that drives our feelings and we can learn how to redirect our thoughts in a more positive way. When experiencing a strong emotion try to restrict your mind from going on a search for a whole long list of other injuries that produced the same emotional reaction. If the emotional expression seems to be dragging on and on, it is because you are allowing your mind to put more and more examples or evidence on the table. You don't want to overwhelm yourself by expressing too much at a time. Allow the emotion. Restrict the thoughts.

The words of poet and former priest, John O'Donohue from his poem, "*For Grief*", reassure us:

> "*...All you can depend on now is that*
> *Sorrow will remain faithful to itself.*
> *More than you, it knows its way*
> *And will find the right time*
> *To pull and pull the rope of grief*
> *Until that coiled hill of tears*
> *Has reduced to its last drop...*"
> (To Bless the Space Between Us, p. 117)

- Sometimes your pain does not reveal itself immediately. You may find it surfaces, to your surprise, months after your actual exit from the cult. You may wonder, *"Why now, when I'm feeling so much better?"* *"Why now, when I've really put some distance between myself and the group?"* Again, the psyche seems to know when to release the pain and how long to allow the expression of said pain. Often it waits until you are feeling stronger and steadier and, once noting that you have acquired the strength to deal with the pain, it allows the pain to come up. If you are too fragile, your psyche will often keep you in a state of denial or distraction until it senses you are strong enough to bear the pain. So if you are feeling a great deal of pain it could very well be that your psyche trusts you are strong enough to deal with it. That's good news! Trust your psyche - it is there to take care of you and will usually do a wonderful job - if you allow it. It's often when we interfere with our body/mind's natural process of healing that we run into problems.

Allow me to summarize by saying that emotion is the way the body/mind reacts to its circumstance and brings itself back to homeostasis (psychological equilibrium). Emotion is designed to move through you and not hang around. When you resist your emotions they have to hang around in your body/mind waiting for an opportunity to be expressed. Your tissue and muscles actually contract and constrict as part of the effort to suppress an emotion. Imagine the amount of tension held in a body that is always contracting to suppress (push down) emotions and then staying tight and contracted to make sure the emotions don't bubble back up. Now that is setting one's self up for dis-comfort and dis-ease.

If you are afraid of your emotional pain and resist it, it seems that inadvertently you turn your legitimate pain into more extreme suffering. Suffering is more intense and more hurtful than pain. Allow yourself to express your feelings, especially via journaling. Expression of some sort is how humans heal from loss, how they grieve, and how they avoid prolonged, unnecessary suffering.

The answer to the question, *"How do I get through all this grief about what I have lost by being a Jehovah's Witness?"*, is: you get through grief by allowing the process of grieving to unfold. There's no magical way around it. Rumi says, *"The cure for the pain is in the pain."* Robert Frost says, *"The only way out is through.*" Humans are wired to grieve for significant losses. Being wired for it, you simply have to allow your body, mind and emotions to feel the pain and mourn the losses. That's the way of it AND there are many sources of help and support for you as you do it. Grieving is the universal and natural process of feeling the pain of loss and then integrating the learnings and meaning of the experience and losses into your life. The grieving process lasts for differing amounts of time with each of us. The price each of us pays for having been in a repressive cult where we cannot be our self and sacrifice our one and only life, is some sort of emotion. Allow the emotion and it moves through you and you heal. Resist it and it sets up shop inside and turns into persistent suffering.

If you have no one to whom or with whom you can express your emotions, use your journal to express. Let your journal become your confidante. Let it be a non-judgmental friend. Writing is a great way to honor your pain and grief as valid, to not resist it, to not become identified with it, and best of all, to not be forever governed by it.

The good news is that not all of your emotions after leaving the cult will be painful. You will surely experience relief, satisfaction, comfort, happiness, anticipation, delight, peace and even joy. Listen to Judith Minty talking about change in her "Letters to My Daughters", "*I give you this to take with you: Nothing remains as it was. If you know this, you can begin again, with pure joy in the uprooting.*" When joy, relief, or satisfaction come, do take time to be totally present to, or 'with' them. Sit with the good feelings. Absorb them. Enjoy them. Write about them. You could also try to imagine, for example, a feeling of joy or delight spreading through your body (in the form of beautiful light, for example), soothing every cell of your being. Soak up all the good. You've had enough of the difficult.

CHAPTER 11

Not Identifying With Negative Thoughts, Beliefs, Feelings or Emotions

Beliefs and emotions, especially ones connected to concepts of God, life, death and eternity seem to become imbedded in our cells. It doesn't seem to work to simply pronounce, "*Well now I've changed my mind*" or "*Now I've seen proof that those beliefs are not true*" and then expect them all to magically and instantaneously dissolve. You may have changed your conscious mind but your unconscious mind may not be quite up to speed. The deeply-imbedded conditioning can still remain tucked in a few corners of your being.

Dreams are often evidence of this. For several years after I had left the Witnesses, in my dreams I would still find myself unhappily planted in the middle of a Kingdom Hall or reluctantly going door-to-door. "*How can this be?*" I wondered. "*I've come to terms with leaving the JWs. I've moved on!*" But clearly my dreams were evidence that *parts* of myself were still stuck back in the cult. That's actually quite normal. Eventually those parts caught up with the conscious choices I had made, but first I had to learn to be patient with myself and accepting of my internal healing process.

It takes time to divest oneself of all the concepts, hopes, fears, patterns and internal programs implanted by a few men in a controlling group, especially if you were in the cult for a long period of time. Be accommodating and understanding with yourself. It's just how the body/mind works.

Take note of old, outdated beliefs that sometimes rise into consciousness but do not identify with them or become upset because they rear their ugly head. It's a normal part of the letting go process. It takes time to leave one belief system, discover what it is we want to believe now, then let go of the old and truly integrate the new.

James Hollis in his book, "What Matters Most", talks about how we need to examine if we are still operating according to someone else's view of reality: *"The implicit, and sometimes explicit, questions our family of origin asked, or our tribe or culture asks, become our questions by default, and we either serve their provisional answers, rebel against them, or try unconsciously to resolve them. Either way we are still in service to someone else's questions, someone else's answers, someone else's unresolved relationship to the universe."* (p.169)

Steve Jobs encourages us to live a life that is our own and not one prescribed by someone else: *"Your time is limited, so don't waste it living someone else's life. Don't be trapped by dogma -- which is living with the results of other people's thinking. Don't let the noise of others' opinions drown out your inner voice. And most important, have the courage to follow your heart and intuition."*

It is important to know that we are all made up of many parts or aspects. For example, you may have noticed yourself saying something like, *"Well a part of me wants to go to the party, but a part of me just wants to stay at home."* or *"I'm of two minds about this."* The field of psychology has different names for our many inner parts, a couple of which are: *"ego-states"* and *"sub-personalities"*.

It may be that even though we are leaving or have left the cult, we have an inner ego-state or subpersonality that is still somewhat attached to the JW dogma and/or the fellowship of the cult. Perhaps we have an inner-child ego-state that only knows itself only as a member of the cult and is afraid it can be punished even more by leaving it. Again, this is all very normal and to be expected. Just remember that there is also a grounded adult ego-state (self) and this is the part of yourself that you want to identify with, operate from, and that you want making the decisions about your new life.

If your scared, JW-attached, inner-child, ego-state makes an appearance in your mind during some moment of vulnerability, reassure him/her that everything is okay, that you've done a lot of research about leaving the organization, that you've thought long and hard about it and are convinced it was/is the right thing to do. Let this conflicted, inner-child ego-state know that the strong, independent, reality-based, adult self is now running your life, that you will not be governed by old patterns, old beliefs, old identities or old fears and it (the scared, inner-child ego-state) must get in the back seat and let the adult you drive the car.

When deprogramming and dealing with conflicted ego-states and/or conflicted beliefs or emotions, a key thing to remember is this:

Relate TO the thought, feeling or ego-state, NOT FROM it:

Relate **to** the fear, **not from** the fear.
Relate **to** the inner-child ego-state, **not from** the inner-child ego-state.

When you relate **to** something you have some distance from it. When you relate **from** something you have no distance, in fact, you are enveloped by it and identified with it, governed by it.

Relating **to** (responding) rather than relating **from** (reacting) could sound something like these following examples:

"I see that I still have remnants of fear in me, and I choose not to be dominated by that fear." (relating TO)
As opposed to "*I'm so scared that I won't be able to cope with being shunned by my family.*" (relating FROM)

"I notice anger simmering below the surface. I am aware that it's there, but I choose not to act from a state of anger right now." (relating TO)
As opposed to "*I'd like to burst into that Kingdom Hall and tell those elders a thing or two!*" (relating FROM)

"I'm aware that a part of me is still feeling depressed even though I am free. I refuse to become identified with these depressed feelings. I choose to live from the parts of me that now know freedom, peace, optimism and joy." (relating TO)

As opposed to "*There's no point to my life now. It has been forever ruined by being a JW.*" (totally identified with the thought/belief, relating FROM it)

"Sometimes I still notice myself feeling like a victim of the WBTS, but I refuse to live or act from that victim ego-state (relating TO)."
    As opposed to "*The Watchtower took so much from me and I'll never recover.*" (relating FROM)

"I can feel a part of me that thinks I should not have made waves and left the organization because of what it has done to my family, but that part of me is very insecure, fearful and feeling 'little'. I am choosing to instead view and manage my life from my grounded, competent, adult self." (relating TO)
    As opposed to "*What have I done? I should never have left the security of my family, the congregation and the organization. I better work to be re-instated.*" (reacting FROM).

When you relate TO your thoughts, beliefs, feelings or ego-states you are, in effect, accepting that they are there and not denying them. When you choose not to relate FROM those feelings, erroneous beliefs or ego-states you are not allowing yourself to become identified with them or driven by them. This is freedom. This is choice. This is health.

Use this technique of "relating to, instead of relating from" to help you remain separate, disidentified and distanced from the thoughts, cult beliefs and ensuing feelings that are vestiges of, or the results of, the old Watchtower programming. Use it to help you not become identified with the symptoms of your pain. This is a really useful technique and it takes some practice to make it your own. Choosing to not identify with the old programming or the beliefs and emotions generated by that old programming can accelerate movement into, and ownership of, your true self, your now JW-free life.

Teacher and author, Stephen Levine suggests another way to not become identified with our suffering or other feeling states is to not even describe them as "*my*" suffering, "*my*" pain, "*my*" sadness (which is "relating *from*") – but to refer to our feeling states as "the" suffering, "the" pain, "the" sadness (which is "relating *to*"). Levine suggests that the pain we are experiencing is a part of the universal experience of suffering, that it is the common pain of all creation and all beings. We do not need to always personalize it or identify it as "mine". Suffering is. If we are human we will know a measure of suffering. That is why we can relate so easily to others' expressions of pain. It is the same pain manifesting in different bodies and minds. Pain is a universal given. Yes, it does sound a bit strange because we are not used to viewing things this way. But if we really want to make sure we do not identify *as, from* or *with* suffering (or any of its multitude components), Levine's suggestion is another viable option for us to consider.

CHAPTER 12

Emotions Manifesting as Physical Ailments

As a current or former member of Jehovah's Witnesses you have had to suppress or repress many of your needs, wishes, impulses, emotions and preferences in order to survive in the cult. Repression and suppression are variants of common psychological defense mechanisms. Defense mechanisms can serve important purposes. Suppression is a more or less conscious choice to forget or force unwanted information out of our awareness. While repression is the unconscious itself acting to keep difficult, double-bind, dissonant and/or hurtful information out of our awareness.

To survive in a cult we had a multitude of things we had to suppress or repress. We had to suppress our doubts, our natural inclinations, our deepest longings. We had to repress our misgivings, our fears, our desires, our feelings (especially rage) and even our true selves. What happens to all this repressed emotional and psychological material? The repressed material doesn't just evaporate. It is buried by the psyche in our body/mind and continues to influence our behaviors and even our physical or mental well-being.

Often things buried or repressed by the unconscious eventually try to come to conscious awareness. If we refuse to or cannot pay attention, the repressed material sometimes manifests as a physical ailment which often symbolizes the contents of the unconscious. Physical ailments that have a psychosomatic origin are not just neurotic figments of one's imagination.

They are ailments in the body (soma) that have their origin in our unconscious or psyche (psyche + soma = psychosomatic). There are hundreds of physical problems that have been shown by years of medical research to be psychosomatic in origin or to have psychosomatic components. Unfortunately, most medical professionals only have the time or inclination to treat the symptom (the physical ailment) and ignore the source (the contents of the psyche).

You may have noticed while you were a Witness, how many of the brothers and sisters are plagued by all manner of physical complaints. Complaints such as backaches, migraines, allergies, chronic pain, chronic fatigue, etc., etc. I had some relatively minor but still debilitating physical problems while a JW and I was definitely not alone. I now see those physical ailments as my body desperately trying to signal me about the many needs and emotions I was ignoring just to survive in the cult. There are some fascinating theories that explain psychosomatic symptomology as well, one of which is the intriguing theory of John Sarno, M.D.

Dr. John Sarno, professor of Rehabilitation Medicine at the New York University School of Medicine, whose specialty is treating people with severe back pain noticed, after much medical testing, that many of his patients had no physical or structural basis for their severe pain and he refused to perform the requested surgery on them. Sarno also noticed that these patients with severe pain, that had no structural basis, had many similar personality traits. Dr. Sarno describes in his book, The Divided Mind (2006) some of the shared traits he noticed in his back pain patients:

- perfectionism
- need to be seen as good (Sarno calls this trait "goodism")
- anxiety, fear
- buried emotional pain
- tendency to feel victimized
- feelings of low self-esteem or self-worth
- demanding of self
- need to feel in control, yet also manifesting some dependency
- having lost a parent

- dominated by a parent (or a parent substitute like JW.ORG)
- guilt
- self-punitive behaviors
- some previous history of psychosomatic complaints
- socially withdrawn

Wow! The above characteristics can definitely be seen in a great number of current or former Jehovah's Witnesses! One could theorize that just being a JW sets one up for physical disorders resulting from those debilitating psychological characteristics as well as all the pressures, double-binds, conflicts and unmet needs that one experiences while a Witness.

Sarno theorizes that people with this strong tendency toward being "good and/or perfect" are also often repressing tremendous amounts of rage (precisely because of the internal pressure created by always trying to be "good"). It would be my guess that most JWs and ex-JWs are full of repressed rage. When the true self has to be deadened in order to survive in a cult, the psyche justifiably becomes enraged.

Sarno claims the perfectionist or "*goodist*" cannot, however, tolerate discovering that he/she is full of rage. If that rage seems to be about to bubble up into conscious awareness, the psyche (unconscious) tries to protect the "*goodist*" person from the rage (and even knowledge of the rage) **by creating a physical symptom to distract them from the content of the unconscious** (undesirable rage) that is threatening to rise into consciousness. The person then becomes preoccupied with the physical symptom and the psyche can again feel safe, as it has distracted the person from knowing about unwanted emotions (especially rage) that would not sit well (creating cognitive dissonance) with their image of themselves as good and perfect.

Sarno says, "*...the psyche views the physical symptom it induces as the lesser of two evils. Better to suffer physical pain than to have one's life ruined by the manifestations of unbridled rage or intensely painful feelings.*" (The Divided Mind, p. 124)

All of Sarno's descriptions apply to my life as a JW and I would bet you find they apply to many of you too. When we have to repress so much of who we are and what we want, it is infuriating to the self.

Trying to be a good, model Jehovah's Witness, we can never reveal the well of anger and rage building inside us – not to other congregation members and, often, not even to ourselves. So the psyche accommodates our need to survive in a restricted environment and our need to maintain our image of our self as good, and represses the rage for us. Then we can continue to go about our JW schedule being perceived as dutiful, remaining in 'good' standing with the organization, and reaping our promised rewards. In fact, the psyche may repress the rage so well that we may even dispute it is there. Perhaps you are disputing or denying your own rage right now!

I would never have described myself as a person full of repressed rage and neither would anyone who knew me! But now I know I was. Perhaps you, too, are thinking, "*Well I'm certainly not an angry person – no one would describe me that way*". May I respectfully suggest you probably are full of unconscious rage for the way you have been treated in the cult – and up until now your psyche has done a great job at protecting you from knowing about that rage. Sarno's theory helped me to understand just how much rage I carried and how the psyche, trying to keep the rage (as well as other feelings and injuries) repressed, caused many of my physical ailments as a distraction. I have used this simple, easy, free (except for the price of a book) Sarno technique with great success for intermittent back pain from which I have suffered for years – probably due to years' worth of repressed rage.

Sarno's latest books suggest that we can use his technique for many more physical ailments than just back pain. I hope this introduction to Sarno's work prompts you to learn more about his medical discoveries and about his simple mind/body prescription for how to eliminate chronic pain, ailments, illnesses. You will learn as much about yourself as you do about his technique! You can read about Dr. John E. Sarno's research, documented 'cures' and prescriptive suggestions in these two books: The Mindbody Prescription: Healing the Body, Healing the Pain, 1998, and The Divided Mind: The Epidemic of Mindbody Disorders, 2006.

So what exactly is Dr. Sarno's mindbody prescription? The prescription that seems to work across the board for a variety of physical symptoms or complaints is summarized below in a much abbreviated form. Don't miss out on the full benefits of the technique by trying to apply my brief summary. Trust me, you need to read his complete prescription, from his books. Sarno suggests that we:

- learn about the psychosomatic process and the psyche's reasons for causing the physical ailment. He originally helped his patients understand his theories by giving free weekly lectures. ABC correspondent John Stossel was one of his clients, as was NYC shock jock, Howard Stern. Stossel did an ABC "20/20" television segment on how he eliminated back pain using Sarno's suggestions (there are YouTube videos of this news segment). We can now simply read Sarno's explanations, his amazing results, and how to apply the method in his above-mentioned book(s)
- inform your unconscious that you know it is causing the physical symptoms, and why
- talk to your brain/unconscious (Sarno provides a detailed script) telling it that you know of its measures to try and protect you from experiencing the rage. (You need the verbatim script from Sarno's books to apply the technique properly.) Once the unconscious becomes aware that you know about its tactic of causing physical pain or illness to distract you from the possible eruption of repressed rage, the tactic, Sarno says, no longer works and the physical symptom should disappear. Magic, or so it seems!
- Sarno's technique does not require you to physically emote or verbally release the rage or any other of the feelings. It seems that just informing the unconscious you know what it is doing and why effects the "cure".

Sarno's non-invasive protocol is quite simple. You do not have to go anywhere to learn it and you can do it while you continue any current conventional treatments for your condition. While there is no guarantee that what you are dealing with is actually psychosomatic in origin and that you will benefit from Sarno's mind/body prescription, it is certainly worth informing yourself and giving it a try.

I would also recommend learning about Eckhart Tolle's concept of "**the pain-body**". Tolle describes the pain body by saying, "*Your story, however, consists not only of mental but also of emotional memory – old emotion that is being revived continuously...most people carry a large amount of unnecessary baggage, both mental and emotional throughout their lives. They limit themselves through grievances, regret, hostility, guilt. Their emotional thinking has become their self, and so they hang on to the old emotion because it strengthens their identity...almost everyone carries in his or her energy field an accumulation of old emotional pain, which I call "the pain-body".*" [1]

It is very easy to hypothesize that Jehovah's Witnesses, both current and former, have very active emotional (and even physical) "pain-bodies". Tolle shares many interesting suggestions on how to dissolve the emotional contents of the pain-body in his books and videos.

Disclaimer: The purpose of shining a light on the works of John Sarno, M.D. is to promote a broad understanding of psychological issues (e.g. psychosomatic illness) that could apply to the situation of current or former cult members. This information is not intended to be a substitute for professional medical advice or treatment. The purpose is to offer psycho-educational insights. Seek the advice of your primary care physician before undertaking any suggestions shared here. Never delay seeking medical help, disregard medical advice, or discontinue medical treatment because of information in a book, including this one. Reliance on any information, suggestions or any recommended resources from this book is undertaken solely at your own risk.

---

[1] A New Earth, Awakening to Your Life's Purpose, 2005, Eckhart Tolle

CHAPTER 13

Accepting Life as it Unfolds

Irish poet, philosopher and former priest, John O'Donohue says, "*I would love to live like a river flows, carried by the surprise of its own unfolding.*" Just as you must work at accepting and allowing your emotions, it is supremely helpful to practice accepting and honoring the flow of your life, as it presents itself. Author, Byron Katie quips, "*You don't get to vote on what is. Have you noticed?*" Life, like a river, flows the way it flows.

This doesn't mean you don't work to heal or you don't develop plans or you don't problem solve or you don't change. It just means for any given moment you do not expend valuable life energy resisting what is. The next moment you may find yourself moving to accomplish something else. That 'movement' then becomes 'what is'. Don't resist the movement to accomplish something. Be present to whatever arises in each moment. Allow it...and then the next moment arrives with another 'what is'. As mentioned before, to be caught in resistance to what is, always produces some form of suffering.

As a reluctant Jehovah's Witness I was always in some form of resistance to what was. I experienced resistance when I had to go in field service, resistance when I had to prepare an assigned talk, resistance when I had to study the Watchtower in order to be able to give a comment from its pages at the meeting. I also experienced discomfort and resistance at many of the things the brothers said from the platform. I wanted to bolt and run when I was assigned to work with brothers or sisters in field service who had issues with physical hygiene or mental acuity. Resistance became almost second nature to me. I disliked 'what was' with regard to all things JW and had a ton of inner opposition, even hostility, about it. Add to that the necessity of keeping this resistance hidden from all the JWs around me and I found myself in an extremely inauthentic, conflicted, unhealthy state. Resistance to 'what was/is' in the present moment became my default position. What a warped, ineffective way to approach life!

Since so much of my life revolved around JW activities I was always wishing each moment could be other than it was. Once out of the cult and once I learned of the psychological and physiological health benefits of accepting life as it unfolds - "non-resistance" - it was a really challenging shift for me to make. Even with the best of intentions I would catch myself resisting life's natural unfolding – always wishing that somehow it could be otherwise. When I noticed the resistance pattern repeating I had to learn to release the resistance and bring my attention back to the present moment and welcome it as it presented itself – "*as a river flows*". Not easy – but oh so worth the effort!

I would encourage you to monitor your thoughts and feelings for a while and notice how often you find yourself resisting what is. Once aware of any pattern of resistance, and now with the awareness of how you can approach life from a alternative, healthier stance, you can then effect the changes.

Your life, my life took a particular path. One of our tasks is to learn to honor the path that brings us to this moment. Can you imagine one day finding value in all the experiences that formed you into the person you are now? It is possible (though not always easy) to arrive at a place where you accept and own all of your life experiences. You may not love all of them, but with time, healing and perspective you can accept them for being part of the river of life that brought you to this precious moment. Wayne Muller in his exceptional book, "Legacy of the Heart" says, *"Accepting the pain we are given requires us to soften our hearts and allow the pain to break us open, to acknowledge and to grieve the terrible sadness that comes with abandonment, loss, illness and disappointment...This is not angry resignation, born of defeat; this is a deep, loving acceptance that what we are given has become our companion and our teacher, regardless of how painful, unwelcome, or unjust."*

What a healing way to reframe the injustices heaped upon us by the leadership of the JW cult. Can you imagine viewing the pain of what you "are given" or have suffered at their hands as your teacher? Ultimately all adversity becomes our teacher. Truly, though we may have difficulty seeing it at first, there is much we can learn from our JW experience and from our pain but first we have to be willing to accept it, be curious about it, and then allow it to instruct us. Once that is done, we can begin to let it go.

If instead, you allow yourself to get stuck in obsessive thinking and a rehashing of the past, forever analyzing your experience and your pain, forever condemning it, forever regretting it, you end up reducing your access to the learning, creativity and energy that helps build a new life. Once you find a peaceful place within where you can accept how your life has unfolded you will have more inner space to access the wisdom, depth and creativity that will propel you into your new life.

A wonderful Zen question asks: *"This being the case, how shall I proceed?"* This question demonstrates acceptance of the situation as it is, and then the readiness to move on to the next thing. *"This being what is (acceptance), how do I go on from here (readiness to move with the flow of life)?"* Beautiful. This is where you want your work of debriefing and grieving to bring you. If, for example, it appears that you will be shunned by key members of your family, you can ask yourself: *"This being the case, how shall I proceed?"* We will each come up with different answers to the question but the value of the question is that it directs our mind away from ruminations about 'the case' (what is). It helps to snap us out of looping thoughts or feelings about what is and shift to thinking about how we can move with the flow of our life. Here are a few specific examples of how you might use, or adapt the above Zen question during and after an exit from the JW cult:

- It now being the case that I have so much more time at my disposal, how shall I proceed?
- It now being the case that my wife wants to remain a JW and I don't, how shall I proceed?
- It now being the case that I have been asked to defend myself before a judicial committee, how shall I proceed?
- It now being the case that I am quite alone after making this decision to leave, how shall I proceed?
- It now being the case that I have my mind, body and life to myself, how shall I proceed?

Using this question helps pull you along with the rhythm and flow of life. It helps you consider the options open to you instead of becoming stuck dwelling on what is 'the case'. When you find yourself stuck obsessively thinking about what is, try to move out of the looping thoughts into how you will proceed with your life, based on what is. How, for example, can you reframe the situation (the "what is") into an opportunity for presence and healing?

Honoring your life as it presents itself to you is also an excellent way to avoid becoming stuck in the stance of a victim. Elizabeth Kubler-Ross says, *"We point to our unhappy circumstances to rationalize our negative feelings. This is the easy way out. It takes, after all, very little effort to feel victimized."*

Yes, if you were caught in a cult you have definitely been victimized. Once out of the cult, feeling rather disoriented and lost for a while, seeing yourself as a victim of the Watchtower organization may be one of the few solid things you have to hang on to. It is human nature to hold onto viewpoints or stances that help us identify where we stand in the world even if they can be counterproductive. But now, in this moment, you have the choice as to whether or not to still think of yourself as the Watchtower's victim. When you are able, try to shift your perspective away from the stance of victimhood to the stance of being free, independent and able. Tich Nhat Hanh says, *"People have a hard time letting go of their suffering. Out of a fear of the unknown, they prefer the suffering that is familiar."*

Preferring our suffering and being the eternal victim of anyone or anything, while deceptively reassuring, can over time be exhausting, disempowering and is never the whole truth of who you are. Listen to the Sufi teacher Pir Vilayat Khan: *"Overcome any bitterness that may have come...Like the mother of the world who carries the pain of the world in her heart, each one of us is part of her heart, and therefore endowed with a certain measure of cosmic pain. You are sharing in the totality of that pain. You are called upon to meet it in joy instead of self-pity."*

One way to recognize that you are caught in the role of victim is when you notice you are feeling a lot of self-pity. Self-pity is a seductive and slippery slope into powerlessness and depression. Invariably, a person stuck in a victim mentality is viewing life through the lens of their inner child. If you find yourself saying *"it's not fair"* a lot, know that that phrase often signals you are approaching life from a child ego-state.

Ideally, you want to approach your new life outside of the cult from a centered, grounded adult stance (ego-state) – not from the point of view of a 'poor-me-Penelope' child. ("Poor-me-Penelope" is a name I gave my inner-child victim who occasionally insinuated herself into my life – until I noticed I had slipped into a moment of self-pity and then purposefully made the shift back to my adult self.) One way to make the shift from a *"poor-me"*, *"not fair"* child-like viewpoint is to confine self-pitying thinking to the thirty minutes of journaling in your "morning pages". Then walk upright and free as your non-victim, adult self for the rest of your day!

The longer you prolong your resentment of the organization that abused you, the longer you remain preoccupied with them, the longer they are still dominating your life and the more likely you are to become listless or depressed. The goal is to name and grieve your losses, to do what is necessary to heal, and to move on to construct a new life. Only you can do this. Irvin D. Yalom says, *"... one is always responsible for the attitude one assumes toward one's burden."*[2] Take responsibility for your viewpoint and stance toward life and refuse to take the attitude that you are the victim of the Watchtower Bible & Tract Society for one minute longer than you need to, to complete your healing!

Author E.M. Forster encourages us to approach important life transitions, *"....not as a victim or a fanatic but as a seafarer who can greet with an equal eye the deep he is entering and the shore he must leave."* What wise advice! You have not truly left the organization behind if you are still nursing resentments and considering yourself a JW victim. Look forward to the day when you no longer view yourself as a victim of the governing body of Jehovah's Witnesses. Look forward to the day when they become irrelevant to your current life and are simply a distant part of your past!

Listen, too, to the sage advice of Stephen T. Butterfield: *"Empowered to turn negativity into a resource... I learned how to crack my habits open and discover the luminous, enlightened energy frozen within them... energy which became available for creative work and joy... I understood that virtues are always cultivated from their opposites: patience is the ability to accommodate impatience, courage is the ability to handle fear, and wisdom is not possible unless confusion is*

---

[2] (Existential Psychotherapy, Irvin D. Yalom, p. 275)

allowed to emerge. Therefore I developed immense respect for my mistakes; without them, my discoveries could not have been made...Any consequence, including betrayal, is a means for waking up."

Following Butterfield's example will help us feel empowered rather than victimized. So many of us have used the betrayals experienced in our relationship with the JW cult as the means of awakening. May we all learn to *"crack the habit of victimhood open and discover the luminous energy frozen within..."* Embark upon the adventure of finding a compassionate solution to your view of yourself as a JW victim. There are so many other more accurate ways to view and define yourself. Don't live your life walking around in shoes too small. They pinch.

As you continue your awakening from indoctrination and enslavement the goal is to move past ruminations about betrayal, past self-pity, past the stance of being anyone's victim. As you begin to feel stronger try to shift your perspective from the mistreatment and the suffering to the ongoing adventure of finding the opportunities and beauty in your current situation.

The Buddha said, *"The root of suffering is attachment."* It's essential to **not** become attached to, or identified with, our suffering as a result of being a Jehovah's Witness. Tara Brach encourages us to instead recognize our suffering as a signal to pay attention, *"Suffering is our call to attention, our call to investigate the truth of our beliefs."* Now that the suffering has your attention, ask yourself if you want to remain the victim of The Watchtower organization. Remind yourself that you have a choice in the matter. When it comes to our attitude, and how we name or label our self or our circumstance we always have a choice.

Be proud that you found the courage and the where-with-all to escape your spiritual, mental and emotional captivity. You decided that the JW cult would victimize you no longer and you left. Remember who you really are and how strong you are. Remember how much you have endured, the strength and the endurance it took just to be a JW. Don't diminish yourself by thinking of yourself as the Watchtower organization's victim. You are so much more than that! As soon as you can, heal the underlying wounds that understandably continue to make you feel victimized. Work to be as free in your mind and heart as you now are in your life!

"See if you can catch yourself complaining in either speech or thought, about a situation you find yourself in, what other people do or say, your surroundings, your life situation, even the weather. To complain is always non-acceptance of what is. It invariably carries an unconscious negative charge. When you complain you make yourself a victim. Leave the situation or accept it. All else is madness." Eckhart Tolle

"Quiet and unnoticed
The flower of your whole life
Has opened its perfect petals."
William Carlos Williams

CHAPTER 14

Who Are You Now, Outside of the Cult?

"Be still ... Listen ... Who are you? Who ... Are You? ..."
Thomas Merton

If you were a Jehovah's Witness for a long time or raised from birth as one as I was, much of your identity has become aligned with, even formed by the incessant indoctrination and constant association with them. Being a member determined what you believed and determined many of your values, preferences and behaviors. In fact, JW doctrines, viewpoints, rules and policies become internalized by their adherents. We become so saturated with their concepts that our true identity has no room to be or to flower.

British pediatrician and psychoanalyst D.W. Winnicott speaks, in his seminal writings on child development, about how humans often build a false self as a necessary defense to cope with an environment that has unreasonable demands and expectations. We can certainly assert that the JW organization has unreasonable demands and expectations! While the false self we build may seem real on the outside because we are always complying with external expectations instead of our own, we can end up experiencing ourselves as empty, phony or dead on the inside. We feel deadened, phony or like an imposter because our true self has been buried by the facade we must build to deal with the invasive demands and unreasonable expectations of external authority figures. These so-called religious authority figures function as a parental substitute for many Jehovah's Witnesses.

The Watchtower organization takes on a strict, parental, authoritarian role in the lives of its members to such a degree that, in order to survive, members have had to bury their true selves, as Winnicott says and live an inauthentic existence from a false self. Sound familiar? It certainly does to me!

The unfortunate bargain we were all pressured to make was to give up our sense of individual identity and autonomy for the promise that we would not be destroyed at the Battle of Armageddon and would live forever on a paradise earth. Time to refuse that ruse. Robert Louis Stevenson said, "*To know what you prefer, instead of humbly saying "Amen" to what the world tells you you ought to prefer, is to keep your soul alive.*"

Note too, what lay sociologist Eric Hoffer says about the pressure within cults and religious movements to suppress or surrender our true self in his seminal book "The True Believer", "*In order to be assimilated into a collective medium a person has to be stripped of his individual distinctness. He has to be deprived of free choice and independent judgment. Many of his natural bents and impulses have to be suppressed or blunted. All these are acts of diminution. The elements which are apparently added -- faith, hope, pride, confidence -- are negative in origin.*" (The True Believer, p. 127)

And then - somehow, some way - you summon the courage to leave the cult. Part of the drive to leave is the call of your true self insisting on finally asserting itself. Part of the discomfort you have felt for so long is because you have been living from a constricted, provisional, false self to survive the demands and pressures of the cult. A good part of your work once out of the cult will be to peel back the layers of that false self and allow your patient, loyal, waiting true self to emerge.

"*I must be willing to give up what I am in order to become what I will be.*" Albert Einstein

"*If a man does not keep pace with his companions perhaps it is because he hears a different drummer. Let him keep step to the music which he hears, however measured or however far away.*" Henry David Thoreau

It will again take time and patience to figure out who you are without the doctrines, without the literature, without the meetings, without the service, without the brothers and sisters, without reliance on the governing body to explain life, God, the world and the future to you. A big part of who you thought you were has, with the act of rejecting their dogma and leaving the cult, disappeared. Carl Jung encourages us with these words, "*The development of personality means fidelity to one's own being.*" Your current quest is a beautiful demonstration of "*fidelity to your own being*" and you must continue to allow the true self to resurface from its protective, hiding place. In his book, "Native Son" (2005), Richard Wright suggests that it is truly a matter of psychological life or death when he says, "*Man can starve from a lack of self-realization as much as ... from a lack of bread.*"

Unfortunately even the disappearance of this false JW self, who you came to believe you were, can for a time be experienced as a loss. Even though you want to eliminate the false self you may still find yourself grieving the loss of it or feeling destabilized as you strip the layers away. You may find yourself asking, "*But, who am I now?*".

The loss of so much of who you thought you were as a JW, including the false self, may for a while be disorienting, distressing and even depressing. This is because you have moved out of familiar environments and patterns. You have left an old comfort zone - even if it was a deep, dark, confining rut. It will take a bit of time for the gloom of missing the old to give way to the brightness of enjoying the new. Don't give up if the gloom continues even when you feel you are doing all the right things. It is to be expected and 'this too shall pass'.

The false self was at the time an appropriate, necessary defense to help you survive in a cult that asked too much of you. Once out of the cult your task is to thank the false self for the protection it provided, tell it you no longer need it now, if necessary mourn its parting, and support the re-emergence of your true self.

"*Everyone must become their own person, however frightful that may be.*" Albert Einstein

As the old false self slides away and the true self slowly emerges you can expect to feel some discomfort. This discomfort does not mean you have made the wrong choice. It simply means that you have crossed a threshold from the old to the new and you have yet to get your bearings. You have to establish new patterns and seek new supports. Since we cannot always count on the availability or fidelity of external supports (people, organizations, groups), we need to concentrate on building our own internal supports. You have to peel back all the layers of indoctrination and control and discover who you are – who you always were – because the greatest support you can find is in allowing your true self to blossom and flower.

"I have lived on the lip
of insanity, wanting to know reasons,
knocking on a door. It opens.
I've been knocking from the inside."
Rumi

In many ways our true self is what we have been looking for all along. We have always had a true self although being a JW required us to bury it. Fortunately it quietly waits for us to remember and recognize it. It does not intrude. Nor does it abandon us. It quietly waits for us. We have been searching for it and, as Rumi suggests, we don't realize that it has always been with us and we have standing beside it and been knocking from the inside! An intimate relationship with the true self was sacrificed to be a JW. We can now open to it, connect with it and encourage it to flower. Actually by leaving the cult we are signaling our psyche that we will no longer live via a false self. We are, without knowing it, heeding the counsel of French philosopher, Jean-Paul Sartre: *"We only become what we are by the radical and deep-seated refusal of that which others have made of us."*

Some ways to encourage the re-emergence of the true self are to:
- always tell yourself the absolute truth
- learn to become your own inner authority
- pay attention to your inner voice
- step out of your child-like self into your adult self
- be willing to compromise, but not to conform (unless you choose to)
- say *"no"* without feeling you have to explain or justify your *"no"*
- listen to your intuition about how to proceed with your life
- honor your curiosity, your right to ask questions and explore
- be willing to face temporary discomfort and pain in service of healing

- be willing to deal with the harsher realities of life
- honor and appreciate your successes and understand your failures
- walk through life with your head up and your shoulders back
- welcome and love your true self unconditionally
- be real, be authentic
- be present and available to yourself

Give yourself the gifts of time, patience and inner support as you work to allow the re-emergence of your true self. You are on the threshold of a powerful transformation where you will discard all the unwanted layers of old, JW identity and discover who you authentically are without the Watchtower's faulty ideological input and invasive controls on behavior. Discover now what YOUR values are, what matters to YOU (your true self), what direction YOU want to take, instead of being a pawn working for the quasi-spiritual but undeniably profit-driven goals of the JW publishing corporation. Carl Jung cautions when creating a vision for a new life that: *"Your vision will become clear only when you can look into your own heart. Who looks outside, dreams; who looks inside, awakes."*

Awakening to who you really are may feel a little intimidating at first but what a magnificent opportunity to reconnect with and restore your real, authentic self. With restoration of your true self in mind here's a little allegory for you:

An Allegory

Imagine for a moment that a precious painting, stolen long ago and hidden in an internationally-known crime syndicate's governing headquarters, has been recovered and brought back to you for restoration. While captive and hanging in the syndicate's headquarters, along with thousands of other stolen masterworks, this masterpiece was not cared for, not attended to, not appreciated as it should have been. In fact, the syndicate's governing-body, in its narcissistic exercise of power, ordered that all the masterpieces in this secretive domain be painted over in order to reflect the syndicate's distorted definition of beauty. They also wanted their syndicate symbol etched here, there and everywhere over the surface of each masterpiece leaving only bits of the original peeking through.

So strokes of off-color, garish paint, not original to the masterpiece, were disrespectfully superimposed on it and all the other masterworks stolen by these unscrupulous thieves. The environment in the headquarters of this syndicate was dark, dank, suffocating - not conducive to the illumination of a masterwork's original face. There was no way for a masterpiece to preserve its original identity and innate dignity. All the stolen masterpieces ended up resembling each other, like clones, with their unique individuality and artistry hidden.

But now, finally, the thieving syndicate is being exposed and many precious stolen masterpieces have been recovered. Some have been reclaimed and returned to their rightful owners. One special painting from among all these abused masterworks has been brought to you for restoration. You alone have been commissioned to take your time and energies to work painstakingly to remove all the layers of gross, offensive deposits not original to it. It is daunting work but knowing how vital it is, you refuse to walk away from the task. With all the strength, determination and skill you can muster you remove the superimposed layers of blasphemy, insult and counterfeit veneer right down to the last intrusive, non-original layer. Finally the pores of the masterpiece can breathe again. What joy you experience as the true colors, textures, depths and nuances of the painting are once again revealed! Finally this masterpiece is all it was originally created to be. The masterpiece has come home ... to itself.

This precious masterpiece is you. After a heroic escape and revival, your masterpiece has at last come home. You were the only one who could bring it home and do the restoration because only you are the curator and overseer of you. You are the only self-governing body who could restore the masterpiece to its original state. What a gift to be able to peel off the deposits of disrespect and darkness and reveal your original identity again. You have reclaimed your true self. The true masterpiece you always were under all the unwanted, superimposed deposits from the crime body is finally free to be and to express itself. (It is only a matter of time before the syndicate's crimes are totally exposed and their confidence game finally collapses on its empty, bankrupt self.)

Social psychologist and psychoanalyst, Erich Fromm, tells us:

> *"The inability to act spontaneously, to express what one genuinely feels and thinks, and the resulting necessity to present a pseudo-self to oneself and others, are the roots of the feeling of inferiority and weakness. Whether or not we are aware of it, there is nothing of which we are more ashamed than of not being ourselves, and there is nothing that gives us greater pride and happiness than to think, to feel, and to say what is ours."* (Escape From Freedom, 1994)

You have reclaimed your treasured masterpiece. Do not leave it uncared for, unappreciated or unsigned.

CHAPTER 15

Let's Talk About Guilt

Whether still inside the JW cult or finally outside of it, you have probably experienced some form of guilt. Guilt is a complicated topic but I want to dissect it a bit here so that you can eliminate any unnecessary guilt picked up from your life in the cult. Guilt is linked to responsibility, feeling we are responsible for something – generally a 'bad' something. There are however, different forms of guilt:

> **Real guilt** comes from an *actual* transgression.
> **Neurotic guilt** comes from an *imagined* transgression.
> **Existential guilt** is a result of feeling we may have transgressed against our very self, especially when we have failed to meet our own potential.
> **Neurotic shame** is a result of a mistaken (imagined) feeling of intrinsic badness or a mistaken impression of the worthlessness of our very being.

Some of our malaise as one of Jehovah's Witnesses may have been due to the ***existential guilt*** of not being able to be authentic, not being free to be our self and reach for our individual potential. Yes, we can actually feel guilt for not being our true self.

The guilt of not realizing our own potential can lead to even more than guilt and despair. Existential psychotherapist, Irvin D. Yalom says, "*The discrepancy between what one is and what one could be generates a flood of self-contempt with which the individual must cope throughout life."* (Existential Psychotherapy, p. 279) Yalom continues speaking about the struggle between our desire for growth and our competing desire for safety, and then talks about American psychologist Abraham Maslow, saying: *"He, too, believed that individuals naturally actualize themselves unless circumstances in their development are so adverse that they must strive for safety rather than for growth "...If the essential...core of the person is denied or suppressed, he gets sick, sometimes in obvious ways sometimes in subtle ways...This inner core is delicate and subtle and easily overcome by habit and cultural pressure...Even though denied, it persists underground, forever pressing for actualization ..."* (Maslow, Psychology of Being, pp. 3-4) *But how is one to find one's potential?. .. Heidegger, Tillich, Maslow, and May would all answer in unison: "Through guilt! Through anxiety! Through the call of conscience!" There is general consensus among them that existential guilt is a positive constructive force, a guide calling oneself back to oneself."* (Irvin D. Yalom, "Existential Psychotherapy", p. 280)

Did you get that? It is such important information. Existential guilt (guilt because you have transgressed against your true self) and its accompanying anxiety is a positive force, a guide, a clarion call to return to yourself. So some guilt you experience may be signaling you that you have actually committed an offense against yourself. You can expunge this kind of existential guilt by softening the defensive armor of your false self and, at long last, establishing a connection to your true self and your true potential. You have already begun that process!

To be members of the Jehovah's Witnesses 'religion', we were required to disconnect from our true selves. We actually ended up alienated from our self. The self signals us to that effect with feelings of discomfort, despair, guilt and sometimes even self-contempt. Our task is then to do whatever it takes to reconnect with our true self and begin the real work of our life – meeting our unique potential as our true self in whatever way that unfolds. Doing that will diminish the discomfort, anxiety, depression and existential guilt. These are things we could not even contemplate doing as one of Jehovah's Witnesses.

By planning to leave the cult, or by having already left, you are heeding the signals of your psyche to come back to yourself, to take back your life and do the work of individuation – of rising to your unique potential. Paul Tillich says, *"...In every act of moral self-affirmation man contributes to the fulfillment of his destiny, to the actualization of what he potentially is."* (The Courage To Be, p.52) So you have already initiated the process of coming back to yourself, of self-affirmation, of realizing your potential!

If instead of heeding the call to come back to our self we are too afraid or too lazy, we may prefer to opt for the seeming security of allowing someone else or something else to make our choices and guide our life. The Watchtower Society is only too willing to step in and take on the task of claiming authority over and managing our life. In fact the price the Watchtower organization demands for offering us the specious opportunity of surviving the Battle of Armageddon and living eternally on a paradise earth is that we surrender our self and our life to them. While accepting such an offer may bring the illusion of security from having to make our own decisions and risking failure, it comes at the terrible cost of despair, disconnection, self-alienation, eventual meaninglessness, disappointment and profound existential guilt (even though we may not be able to name it as such at the time).

Existential guilt can serve as a healthy guide back to ourselves but ***neurotic guilt*** is not nearly as healthy! Religions actually encourage neurotic guilt by accentuating that we are born sinners (habitual sinners) in need of redemption mediated by their unique intercessions and sometimes by means of works prescribed by them. Religions teach us to feel bad if we refuse their ministrations and it follows that when we imagine we have done something 'wrong' we feel guilt – neurotic guilt. Remember, neurotic guilt is about an imagined transgression not a real one.

If guilt about leaving the JW 'religion' is one of the feelings you are experiencing you need to take some time to examine it closely. Try to determine exactly what it is that you have done that is wrong. Is it really wrong to change your mind? Is it really wrong to do research and once you have discovered serious errors and deceptions to decide to leave and change course? (Is that not what the apostle Paul did when he left the Jewish faith to follow Christ? How is it that millions have the right to change their minds to become Jehovah's Witnesses but Jehovah's Witnesses do not have the right to change their minds and leave JW.ORG without being punished?) Is it wrong, once you have discovered your options as an adult have been seriously limited by religious indoctrination, to decide to leave an organization? The answer is a resounding "NO".

If you are experiencing guilt in spite of being able to answer "no" to the above questions, the guilt is not real and is not yours to bear. The guilt you experience about exiting the cult is due to an implanted, imaginary transgression. It has been programmed into you with the JW's insidious indoctrination in the hope that the guilt will keep you under their control and caught in the cult. There is no real transgression and the guilt you feel is not real. It is unhealthy, neurotic guilt. Make sure your self realizes that you are not guilty of any such imaginary transgressions!

Real guilt emerging from the conscience is a signal to a human that they have done something wrong and need to address the situation. If we have done something wrong we need to make amends if we can and apologize to anyone who may have suffered as a result of our action (s). If neither of these steps can be taken, it could be that your guilt is guilt that has been put on you – that is imagined. Real guilt, however, is a call from our conscience to pay some serious attention to what we are doing or have done.

It is important not to let neurotic guilt (or real guilt for that matter) hang around in your mind. Let me explain why: In the god-like, parental, sometimes punitive, part of our mind that Freud named the "Superego", **feelings of guilt always demand punishment**. As well, our western culture has the 'original sin' template from the Garden of Eden story deeply imbedded in our minds. That template and other Biblical stories stress that the guilty sinner must be punished. If the sinner is not punished immediately the Bible always promises future punishment. If you are feeling guilty your Superego function can assume you have sinned and are, therefore, in need of punishment. Psychologists believe that some accidents and illnesses are the result of an unconscious, neurotic need for punishment.

By allowing a guilty feeling to persist in you, you can inadvertently be setting up the creation of unconscious impulses for self-punishment. The punitive Superego takes on the task of meting out the punishment and so, in effect, you end up *unknowingly* punishing yourself. Get rid of any guilt for imaginary transgressions and thereby remove the Superego's impulse to punish! You are already being punished enough by the governing body for daring to heed the call of your true self!

Existential psychiatrist, Irvin D. Yalom writes, "*Following Freud, two generations of analysts developed the field of psychosomatic medicine in which a number of medical illnesses (for example, arthritis, ulcers, asthma, ulcerative colitis) were discovered to be powerfully influenced by a patient's psychological state.*"(Existential Psychotherapy, p. 273) Don't let **neurotic guilt** become a lingering part of your psychological state. As said, you have already suffered enough unjust and unwarranted punishment instigated by the Watchtower organization. Get rid of any unhealthy neurotic guilt so that your super-ego does not create any additional forms of self-punishment (e.g. depression, failures, accidents, chronic pain, illnesses, chronic anxiety, self-sabotage, etc.).

You are not committing a sin to leave the Watchtower organization. You are not committing a sin because you change your mind. You are not bad. You have not transgressed any laws. You do not need to feel guilt and you certainly do not need to be punished!

If you are feeling guilty remind yourself, over and over again, that you are not guilty of any real transgression even though the Watchtower Society wants you to believe that you are. If you are feeling guilt about leaving the organization tell yourself it is guilt about *imaginary* transgressions not real ones. Every human has the right to decide what they will do and what they will not. You are simply exercising your basic human rights.

In summary, if you notice a feeling of guilt consider what might be causing it. If you know you have made a *real* transgression correct it and/or make amends. Apologize to any injured party and then *let it go*. Remember the ancient Biblical template by which our superego operates. It believes guilt needs punishment. So don't let a feeling of guilt even for a real transgression hang around too long in your mind. Do what you can to correct the situation and then let go of real guilt, too. If you have deeds in your past that you are not proud of and you have done what is possible to correct them you must then *forgive yourself* for those behaviors and move on. The best way to eliminate long-standing guilt for past errors of commission or omission is to forgive yourself. **Forgive yourself** for all the ways you may have been insensitive, selfish, inattentive, unavailable, etc. The statute of limitations for feeling guilty about and punished for past failings is up. You signal this to your body/mind by forgiving yourself.

If, as you reflect upon a feeling of guilt you determine it is not connected to a specific real or an imaginary transgression then consider that it could be that clarion call of existential guilt we talked about earlier. Recall that the existential guilt and attenuating feelings are urging you to no longer ignore your right to be all you can be. Every Jehovah's Witness transgresses against the inner imperative to be all they can be when they surrender their self, their mind, their life to the agenda of the Watchtower Bible & Tract Society. Step away from this unhealthy relationship that is keeping you from connecting with your true self and developing your innate potential. Don't wait for permission to make your next move in life. Seize your one and only life now. As you do, existential guilt should begin to disappear.

Will you transgress against the healthy inner summons to meet your potential, by abandoning your true self while submitting to the directions of an external parental substitute? Will you transgress against your own destiny when you do not listen to the inner voice that urges you to walk through all inner and outer barriers toward freedom and meaning? Please say "*No!*"

Shame

Just for clarification, it is important to know that guilt and shame are very different things. **Guilt** is about feeling we have *done* something wrong or bad. **Shame** is about feeling we *are* something wrong or bad. Guilt is about doing. Shame is about our being. No young human intrinsically feels shame, whereas their healthy conscience will push them to feel guilt if they have done something wrong.

We usually absorb shame from some sort of negative external treatment. Real guilt is an inner prompt to correct a situation whereas shame serves no purpose other than to pull us down into depression and low self-esteem and to make the person or organization who shamed us feel righteous and morally superior. Real guilt arises from the conscience of a person, whereas shame is usually put on a person by another. Some of us may later take on the task for them, and actually start shaming ourselves.

No matter what rule the JW organization says you have transgressed, you are not guilty of any death-worthy offense and you certainly are not shameful. Your being is not shameful. Your impulses, needs and human drives are not shameful. This applies whether you have engaged in casual sex, stolen something, are bisexual, have told lies, are prejudiced, masturbate, have watched pornography, have wished someone ill, have had an orgasm while being sexually abused, had to leave your children behind with the JW parent, etc., etc., etc. If you have internalized all the Witness interdictions about basic human needs, desires and behaviors, it is easy to slip into shaming yourself. The Witnesses would not accept you as a normal, imperfect human being, so YOU must now accept your needs, impulses, preferences, mistakes - your crazy, quirky, learning and growing self - as you are! You may rightly feel the need to condemn and correct particular *behaviors* now and then, but you must **never condemn your very *being***.

The way the JW organization treats members who decide to leave is designed to induce shame in us and a feeling of self-righteousness in themselves. Their hope is that we will return to the fold with our tail between our legs. Being ordered to appear in front of a judicial committee as if we have committed a crime, being told we are ousted from God's "only true organization", having it publically announced at a meeting that we are disfellowshipped, that no one should associate with us, having the congregation told that we have engaged in "conduct unbecoming a Christian", and then having JW members of our very own family cut us off, is all designed to shame us. Often we leave the cult feeling deeply shamed. Slough off the shame they put on you.

Shame heaped upon you from JW.ORG is not yours to bear, or believe. Such shame comes to you from the reprehensible, contrived concepts of a self-righteous governing body and the unfortunate thing is that you (we) take it on. If you are still stuck with unnecessary shame from JW.ORG, you must rid yourself of it as soon as possible. Remember, we sometimes make errors of conduct, but we can never make an error of being. No matter what you have done, no matter what you have thought, no matter what you have wished in the deepest recesses of your being, **you have a right to be here**. You have a right to follow your inner knowing and leave a cult, a religion, a destructive relationship, etc.

If shame is an issue for you, it could prove helpful for you to say something like the following sentences to yourself:

"There is a part of myself that feels shameful, but I, my true self, knows my being could never be shameful. I am a normal, flawed, yet lovable human being with every right to walk this planet. There were times in life when I knew nothing of shame. I'm going to recall those shame-free times now."

"There is a part of myself that has internalized the insults and insinuations of external forces from my past but I, my adult self knows those insults and insinuations are not the truth of who I am. The insults are not mine to bear. I choose to eject them from my mind and heart!"

"There is a part of myself that feels shameful, but my true self knows I, my very being, could never be shameful. The actions and insinuations that made me feel shame were injurious. My adult self now chooses to reject the shame and heal any injuries left by that unwarranted shaming. I am freeing myself, now and forever, of any vestiges of JW shaming!"

"There's a place in the soul where you've never been wounded." Meister Eckhart

"If we can share our story with someone who responds with empathy and understanding, shame can't survive." Brene Brown (Daring Greatly)

CHAPTER 16

Dealing With: Differences – Ruminations – "Shoulds"

While there will be many commonalities in the stories of ex-JWs' experiences in the cult, exiting the cult, and adjusting to life outside of the cult, there will also be *differences*. Take my husband and myself as an example. We sometimes find ourselves recalling a trip to a convention, listening to a public talk by a member of the governing body, or reading about 'new light' in the Watchtower, etc. and though we agree on the details of the event, our reactions to it, both at the time and even now can be very different.

As I compare our reactions I see that my husband took much of the mind control, the undue influence, the required isolation from 'the world' much less to heart than I. While his less reactive stance can be due to many factors (ego strength, gender, age, character development, perceptions, interpretations, childhood vulnerabilities, etc.) there is something I (and perhaps you) can learn from him. What I have learned from him is not to take everything the governing body required of us, imposed upon us, denied us, did to us, quite so personally. I know - easy to say! However the more personally we take their imposed ideology, rules, pressure, the more personally we take their deceptions and betrayals, the more wounded we will feel and the longer we will spend nursing and healing those wounds. I offer myself as proof of that. Don't follow my example!

Even though my husband and I lived together as Jehovah's Witnesses for years, we had quite different experiences in the JW organization. As a woman I was at the bottom of the ranking in the JW pyramid. A woman's role is to be an obedient, submissive, regular publisher of the good news of the Kingdom. Women are to consider it a privilege to sit at the meetings and lap up all the spiritual food fed to them by their superior brothers. Women are given no congregational responsibilities and can take no initiative to do anything in the congregation (except clean the bathrooms and help with crying babies). Women can, however, feel free to take the initiative to help and encourage other women as part of their Christian "privileges". Women must also never find themselves in the position of teaching a man. The result of all of this is, as I see it, that women end up bored out of their minds as one of Jehovah's Witnesses. If you are a female in this cult, you get to dance to the tune of a 'one-note samba' (no variations, no pirouettes, no leaps, no twirls, no dips, no solos, no spins, etc.) for the rest of your life.

Men, on the other hand, have many seemingly desirable tasks they can aspire to in the congregation. They are assigned responsibilities from a whole specter of "privileges" that require them to study, research, prepare talks, arrange demonstrations, travel from congregation to congregation to deliver public talks, teach from the platform, "shepherd the flock", co-ordinate large conventions, help with the design of new kingdom halls, oh... and make sure women remain in submission to their husbands, etc., etc.

My husband enjoyed studying and preparing talks for meetings, for circuit and district assemblies, and he was good at it. He managed the department at District Assemblies that looked after security and seating arrangements for the conventions and was always praised for his efforts. As an elder he was involved in problem-solving, 'counseling', organizing, overseeing "judicial hearings", correspondence with Bethel, scheduling, etc. etc. He was often called on to preside as the minister at weddings and as master of ceremonies at wedding receptions. He was also called upon to use his speaking skills and empathic ministrations as he presided at funerals.

My husband's male-only privileges called upon some of his talents such as his public speaking and his organizational abilities. He had the satisfaction of using his competencies and seeing congregations prosper and conventions proceed because of his efforts. As he did all this, I had the privilege of tagging along and sitting in the audience bored, frustrated and angry passing the time by daydreaming about projects I had at home and things I hoped to accomplish in the future.

Men are challenged and rewarded for stepping up and working in the JW congregation. Women are not. Women get to sit unchallenged during the meetings and engage in encouraging banter with other witnesses after the meeting. What more could a lowly female of the species aspire to? Women's talents and competencies go unnoticed, unrequired, unused and unappreciated. The air in the Kingdom Hall wafted with misogynist fumes. I literally got to the point where I felt so stifled, constrained, repressed, frustrated and furious that I thought I might physically implode and if there would not have been huge unpleasant repercussions for myself and my husband it would have been very satisfying to verbally explode! All that to say, my husband has some good memories of being a member of the JW org. Men are noticed, required, used and appreciated and may even miss the challenges and appreciation when they leave the organization. Apart from a few rewarding relationships with people, I do not have good memories of my years stagnating as a Witness. My husband and I have had to learn to allow for, understand and appreciate our differing perceptions based on very different experiences in the cult.

Ultimately, it serves no great purpose to debate whether it is more challenging to be a male Witness or a female Witness; whether it is harder to leave the cult when you are young or more mature, male or female, born into the cult or converted. Suffice it to say each JW story and exit experience will be *different* based on factors such as gender, age, race, marital status, education, personality traits, resources, etc. What is not different is the bitter taste of deception, betrayal, injustice, hurt and anger left in our mouths once we do leave.

> *"Don't let your luggage define your travels, each life unravels differently."*
> ~Shane Koyczan

Another way to remain caught in JW wounds is by *excessive rumination* about them. Try not to get stuck in a pattern of obsessively reviewing, mulling over, remembering all the pressures, abuses and humiliations you experienced in the cult. It keeps you tied to the cult, keeps the wounds open and oozing and does not help you get on with the creation of a new life of your own.

Rumination is a normal thing to do right after any traumatic event, but once you have some distance try not to let your thinking pull you back into forever licking your wounds. 'Licking' wounds keeps them open. That's why veterinarians often put a huge, plastic collar around the neck of a dog or cat that has just had an operation. They want to prevent the animal from obsessively licking its wounds, as compulsive licking prevents the incision from healing. Don't prevent your psychological and spiritual wounds from healing by being excessively absorbed ruminating about them.

Unfortunately, I speak from experience when it comes to excessive rumination. I wasted way too much precious time dwelling on all the 'what-ifs' and coulda, shoulda, woulda scenarios. This is not helpful or healthy. It is toxic, keeps you stuck, and prolongs your suffering.

If you, too, find yourself thinking a lot of *"should" thoughts* such as:

- "I should write to the Society itemizing all their abuses."
- "I should tell Dad about all the JW.ORG deceptions."
- "I should get rid of all the Watchtower literature in my home."
- "I should join in the activist work against the Watchtower."
- "I should get involved with another religion right away."
- "I should listen to what my JW friends think of me now."
- "I should consider doing what is required to be reinstated."

then here is a quick way to reframe these statements and take a little pressure off of yourself: **Change the word "*should*" to "*could*" and at the end of the new sentence with the word "could", add the phrase "*and I have a choice*".**

Okay, let's try this quick and effective technique on the above 'should' sentences:

"I *should* write to the Society itemizing all their abuses."

Change to: "*I **could** write to the Society itemizing all their abuses, **and I have a choice.**"*

"I *should* tell Dad about all the JW.org deceptions."

Change to: "*I **could** tell Dad about all the JW.org deceptions, **and I have a choice.**"*

"I *should* get rid of all the Watchtower literature in my home."

Change to: "*I **could** get rid of all the Watchtower literature in my home, **and I have a choice**.*"

"I *should* join in the activist work against the Watchtower."

Change to: "*I **could** join in the activist work against the Watchtower, **and I have a choice**.*"

"I *should* get involved with another religion right away."

Change to: "*I **could** get involved with another religion right away, **and I have a choice**.*"

"I *should* listen to what my JW friends think of me now."

Change to: "*I **could** listen to what my JW friends think of me now, **and I have a choice.**"*

"I should consider doing what is required to be reinstated."

Change to: *I **could** consider doing what is required to be reinstated, **and I have a choice**.*

Did you notice when you read the "*could*" and "*and I have a choice*" sentences how much more of a free, liberated feeling you have? By making that simple adjustment in your wording, you remind yourself you have options. You can choose one way or you can choose another way. You are free. (The above technique works less well if you are changing a "should *not*" to a "could *not*". It works best for a simple change of "should" to "could", using the present tense.)

Living as Jehovah's Witness programmed clones we were brainwashed into giving up any sense of power to make our own choices. We forgot we could look for other options. We forgot there was such a thing as alternatives. Reclaim your inborn right to make your own choices. Reinforce your right to reflect upon the options in any given situation and make your own considered decision. Refuse to be pressured, duped or conned into submission and subjection by JW.ORG any longer! Watch out as well for the tyranny of your own internal 'should' thoughts.

"...there are moments when one has to choose between living one's own life, fully, entirely, completely – or dragging out some false, shallow, degrading existence that the world in its hypocrisy demands. You have that moment now. Choose!"
~Oscar Wilde

"May your choices reflect your hopes, not your fears."
~Nelson Mandela

CHAPTER 17

Suggestions for Healing from Effects of Cult Control

Take Charge of How You Direct Your Attention

Our attention is one of the most powerful and precious resources we have. We tend to employ the word 'attention' rather casually. But how we direct our attention determines our experience and ultimately the quality of our life. Professor of psychology and education at the University of Chicago, Mihaly Csikszentmihalyi tells us, "*The more psychic energy we invest in a painful event, the more real it becomes...*" (Finding Flow, p. 128) It is with our attention that we invest our life energy. How are you using your precious life energy? Are you using it to ruminate, regret, rehash? What if you chose to redirect your attention – redirect it to a current personal project, or what is good in your life now, rather than keeping it trained upon the betrayals and disappointments of the past?

I don't recall where I heard this but these few words have never left me: "*Attention is an act of love.*" It's true, isn't it? We demonstrate our interest in and love for someone or something with our attention. Attention is the loving gift of our precious energy. We demonstrate what matters to us by where and how we direct our attention. What does it say then if we allow much of our attention to be focused on the deceptions, disappointments and losses of our life? How much more adaptive and beneficial to direct our attention to our life now and all the possibilities it holds. How much wiser to direct our attention where we can still have some influence. When you catch yourself with your attention on the past or on the JW abuses, take a deep breath and pivot your attention to something that will contribute to your life now.

Csikszentmihalyi in his book "Finding Flow: The Psychology of Engagement with Everyday Life" encourages us to "*selectively ignore painful situations*" in order to find creative flow in the present moment. It is really counter-productive to allow your attention to always be focused on the ways you were held back or hurt by the JW cult. Your attention is yours to direct. Don't allow it to continually drift back to them and what they took from you. Don't let them hijack your aliveness or consciousness for one moment longer than you need to heal. Political activist and author, Susan Sontag said, "*Do stuff...be curious. Not waiting for inspiration's shove or society's kiss on your forehead. Pay attention. It's all about paying attention. Attention is vitality.*"

Selectively direct your attention to that which will benefit your healing from the spiritual abuse and to that which will help you build your new life.

Be Willing To Experience Discomfort

We all want to be comfortable but when we make big changes in our lives we lose a certain level of comfort and it takes time to establish a new comfort zone. Do not allow yourself to slip back into old, counter-productive but comfortable zones of operation. You have made a big change that has pulled you away from habitual beliefs, patterns and activities. Expect to, and be willing to, feel some discomfort as you leave these habitual patterns of thinking and acting behind. The discomfort will eventually pass as you create a new life and a new comfort zone in it. Expect to eventually experience a glorious comfort in your hard-won freedom - but not immediately. Remind yourself that temporary discomfort is evidence of the huge change you have made. Allow it and it will soon pass.

If your main (and perhaps unconscious) priority is safety and comfort you will find it very hard to make a major change in your life. You have to be willing to temporarily experience discomfort and uncertainty when you enter a new phase of life. Sometimes we try to avoid the discomfort of change and even the discomfort involved in healing by resorting to a sort of intellectual quest to discover all the reasons for our problems, pain or abuse. While some intellectual understanding of what happened to us is definitely required, we need to make sure that we don't use our need to *know* (and thereby stay comfortably in our head) as a way to avoid the need to *feel*, in order to heal.

Wayne Muller says, *"This preoccupation with discovering the reasons behind the...injustices can sometimes blind our hearts to the tremendous opportunities for healing and liberation available to us in this very moment. But it is so difficult for us to let go of the search for the answers to the questions: Why...? Why me? We pick at the scabs and scars in our heart, waiting for an answer that may never come. We would rather explain our hurt than feel it."* (Legacy of the Heart, p. 4)

Intersperse the need to understand the cult experience and its effects with the necessary discomfort of recognizing, allowing and expressing feelings about the spiritual, physical, and emotional abuse. Intellectual explanations and understanding can provide a comforting distance and distraction from our actual experience (which is often a form of psychological resistance), but we have to find the courage to also take up the real work of healing by being willing to feel, and thereby heal, what we had to suppress for so many years.

"The only way that you'll actually wake up and have some freedom is if you have the capacity and the courage to stay with the vulnerability and the discomfort." Tara Brach

Learn To Reframe Your Experiences

Shift your perspective. For example, if you are being shunned by family and friends you will experience moments of feeling very alone. When you can, try to reframe the aloneness into being an opportunity instead of a curse. Remind yourself that this period of aloneness allows you the opportunity to recover from the abuses of the cult and uncover who you are now. If you were busy with all the activities that the Society, families and friends require it would take much longer to do this deeply personal and introspective work of healing and recovery.

Mizuta Masahide, a Japanese poet from the seventeenth century gives us a beautiful example of a reframe: *"Barn's burnt down, now I can see the moon."* It's all a matter of where we decide to direct our attention, isn't it?

Can you make it a point to direct your attention to what is positive in your current situation?

Existential psychiatrist and Holocaust survivor, Viktor E. Frankl wrote the seminal book "Man's Search For Meaning". In the death camps during the Second World War he lost his wife and every other member of his family, except his sister. His expressions on how to continue living after experiencing such inhumanity and immense loss are full of wisdom. He suggests that we 'reframe' our thinking or adjust our attitude. Here are a few quotations by Frankl that have helped me over the years:

> *"Everything can be taken from a man but one thing: the last of the human freedoms – to choose one's attitude in any given set of circumstances, to choose one's own way."*

> *"Between stimulus and response, there is a space. In that space is our power to choose our response. In our response lies our growth and our freedom."*

> *"Forces beyond your control can take away everything you possess except one thing, your freedom to choose how you will respond to the situation."*

> *"To suffer unnecessarily is masochistic rather than heroic."*

What powerful, helpful reframes by Frankl! Listen to the way British playwright, Tom Stoppard chooses to frame new beginnings: *"It makes me so happy. To be at the beginning again, knowing almost nothing ... It's the best possible time of being alive, when almost everything you thought you knew is wrong."* Now that's a reframe!

Fear-Based or Love-Based?

Rank and file Jehovah's Witnesses are trained by the JW organization to be governed by fear. Fear pervades, in some way, almost every public talk, almost every Watchtower article, almost every exhortation of members of the governing body on JW.ORG broadcasting, etc. The governing body of Jehovah's Witnesses bullies, intimidates and even terrorizes their members with both subtle and not-so-subtle threats of what will happen if they don't follow the rules. This intimidation manifests as fear in the follower and that fear that produces the desired submission and obedience. The governing body teaches its followers to be afraid of a myriad of things, such as: Satan, the demons, destruction at Armageddon, churches, worldly associations, pagan customs, pagan symbols, pagan celebrations, apostates, phallic symbols, apostate literature, worldly music and films, higher education, blood transfusions, missing meetings or service, disfellowshipping, being shunned, being barred from paradise, etc.

As a Jehovah's Witness fear invariably becomes a major motivator. Fear is used to keep you off-balance, needy, submissive, afraid, obedient and loyal. Yes, the Society says they have created a loving community of brothers and sisters and there are many moments when we enjoyed apparent loving association. But what happens to that love if you question the governing body's decisions? What happens to that love if you ask for clarification about a doctrine? Where does that love go if you say you want to leave their ranks? The love in the organization is totally conditional. The love is there if you are obedient and unquestioning. The governing body rarely motivates its followers to action with love. Fear is the coin of their realm.

All that to say, when we leave the Jehovah's Witnesses we invariably leave as a person who is fear-based – a person who is permeated with, and governed by, many fears. Fear has often become the default position from which we think, decide and act. If we live our life from a position of fear we are setting ourselves up for anxiety, paralysis, pain and suffering. If we can re-learn how to live our life from a stance of love, life becomes much easier, more satisfying, open, expansive and skillful.

If you are living from a position of fear, your body, mind, life is: constricted, tight, closed, limited, preparing for fight, flight or freeze, defensive, often paralyzed or stuck, full of worry, full of anxiety, full of dissatisfaction.

If you are living from a position of love, your body, mind, life is: open, relaxed, expansive, welcoming, sensitive, attentive, curious, understanding, skillful, able, compassionate, and content.

As you proceed with your new life outside of the JW cult you do not want to drag the fear-based thinking, deciding and acting with you. Easier said than done, I know. When you find yourself in a challenging situation, or experiencing difficult feelings, try asking yourself the following questions:

How would this issue, decision, problem, memory or situation be different if I approached it from a position of love rather than a position of fear?

How would I think, feel or behave differently in this circumstance if I approached it from a place of love (of self, other, or life) rather than a place of fear?

When you shift your stance from a fear-based one to a love-based one your perspective softens, opens and expands. Love of life, self, others and the planet opens your vision to a higher level of thinking and, therefore, opens your heart and mind to new possibilities. Best of all love is a much more comfortable place from which to live.

I often use one of the above questions, or a version thereof, when I notice I feel stymied or distressed by a memory, decision or situation. *How would this situation be different if I approached it from a position of love instead of fear?* It still astonishes me how often I am unaware that I am viewing a decision or situation from a place of fear and need to make the shift to love. And oh my, how the shift from fear-based thinking to love-based thinking changes everything!

"Under any religion, the pre-established impersonal code transcends the right of the individual to explore, experience, and marvel at the mysteries of his own life and death. Religions introduce us not to God but to slavery. They deprive us of our freedom to explore our own souls and to discover the endless and wondrous possibilities presented to us by an infinite universe. And most often the method of religions is fear, not love. They demand blind obedience and often obedience to dreadful dogma." Gerry Spence, Lawyer

Don't Believe Every Stressful Thought You Think

Truth be told, most of our stressful, judgmental and fearful thoughts are not entirely true. Rudyard Kipling said, "*Of all the liars in the world, sometimes the worst are your own fears.*" Don't buy into every fearful thought you think about what 'this' might mean, or 'that' might mean. Be willing to challenge the thoughts that cause you pain. After you notice yourself thinking a stressful or discouraging thought stop and ask yourself, "*Is that **really** true?*", "*Is that completely true?*" You will be surprised how many times the answer will be "*no*". Having challenged the stressful thought and discovered it is not the whole truth, let it go and replace it with a truthful, kinder, gentler, stress-free, love-based thought.

You may find "*The Work*" of teacher Byron Katie helpful when it comes to challenging stressful thoughts. Katie suggests writing down stressful thoughts on worksheets and asking four questions about them, beginning with "*Is that true?*" Visit Byron Katie's website at www.thework.com. She has the worksheets there, and you can download them for free. You will also find videos of Katie doing 'the work' with people on a variety of issues where she helps them challenge stressful and painful thinking. One of Byron Katie's books is "Loving What Is" (2003). In it Katie says: "*You don't have to believe everything your thoughts tell you ... become familiar with the particular thoughts you use to deprive yourself of happiness.*"

When you notice yourself caught by repetitive, looping, negative thinking that you just can't seem to shake, and that is depriving you of happiness, try to identify the specific thought that is distressing you. As above, you can question the truth of it, *and* you can go a layer deeper. Try asking yourself what is the hidden belief underneath the stressful thought. What is the belief that gives the stressful thought life? Then test the belief to see how true it is. I used questions to test the veracity of beliefs all the time with my therapy clients. Questions such as:

- How accurate is that belief?
- Is that your belief, or one inherited from an outside source?
- What would your life be like if you let go of that belief?

- Who would you be without that belief?
- In order to feel better, are you willing to give up that belief?
- What would be a healthier, more skillful thought or belief?
- What would be a less fear-based belief?

Any time you find yourself suffering, take a look at the underlying beliefs that are driving your thinking. Often the beliefs are just as mistaken, outdated and as unnecessary as the stressful thoughts. Release the old erroneous, pain-inducing thoughts and beliefs and enjoy the relief and peace that flood in as a result.

Try Not To Catastrophize or Dramatize Your Situation

Stick to the facts, unless you are specifically wanting to explain how certain events affect you on an emotional level. Here's an example of catastrophizing: "*I just cannot survive being shunned by my family.*" Is that a fact? Is it really true that you cannot survive the shunning? A more factual and less catastrophizing statement would be: "*I'm finding it really painful to be shunned by my family.*" The truth is you will survive the shunning, it just won't be easy. Don't frighten yourself by catastrophizing. Speak only the truth to yourself.

It perhaps seems like a small thing, but your body/mind (and perhaps your fearful inner child) is listening as you think or say catastrophizing or dramatizing things and contracts and quakes with fear as a result. We want to minimize the stress and any psychological and physical constriction you experience. You can again use the techniques of Byron Katie with catastrophizing thoughts. Ask yourself, "*Is that really true?*" It usually isn't. Then find the truth and modify the statement to reflect what is true. When thinking about (or talking about) your injuries and losses try not to exaggerate for effect. The effect may be one you don't want – that of raising your anxiety and sense of woundedness.

You've been through enough stress exiting the cult. Don't add to it by overly dramatizing the specifics of your experience (past or present) with the way you think or talk about it. Stick strictly to the facts. Omit the drama. Leave out the exaggerations. Catastrophizing and dramatizing can be re-traumatizing! Refuse to participate in re-traumatizing yourself and perhaps thereby depressing yourself.

Although you are not entirely responsible for your servitude to the Watchtower organization, you are now entirely responsible for the attitude (which includes what you think, believe and say) you adopt toward that period of your life. It may take some concentrated work, for a time, to create a few necessary adjustments in how you think about and talk about your wounds. Those adjustments can greatly reduce your distress, suffering and level of depression. Don't become trapped or traumatized by the stories you tell yourself about your life.

Make Wise Use of Your Extra Time

Now that you are not attending meetings, not having to read Watchtower literature, and not devoting time to spreading their kingdom message, you have reclaimed many hours back into every week. If you are being shunned by family and friends you have even more time to yourself that you did not have before. Don't allow these reclaimed hours to be simply filled with regret, bitterness and loneliness. Find ways that please you to fill the time. For example:

1. Take a course to learn something you've always wanted to do – a specialty cuisine, photography, languages, sports, music lessons, meditation, etc.
2. Form a group or workshop to teach something from your unused bank of talents and expertise.
3. Reclaim your right to read all the great literature you've missed.
4. Reclaim your right to enjoy the all the great music you've missed.
5. Take an art history or art appreciation class.
6. Volunteer – there are so many worthy causes.
7. Make yourself an expert in something you have always been interested in, by engaging in some serious research and study.
8. Jump-start your new life by engaging in *Bibliotherapy* (reading quality self-help books).

9. Write weekly notes or letters to family or friends who are required to shun you. (Keep the notes kind and love-based, without using shaming or 'guilting' language.) Tell them about your life and your on-going love for them. You may choose not to mail the letters because they will probably not be read. If you keep them, you will have them to share (if you choose) with your loved one if/when they awaken from the spell of the cult.

I have no doubt that you can add to this list with things you have always wanted to explore or do. The above list is offered to help get you thinking about ways you could productively use your extra time. The mind does not like a vacuum. If you do not fill your time and mind with stimulating activities and enriching material, you may find yourself wallowing in hurt and self-pity that will happily rush in to fill the empty spaces.

"Time is the coin of your life. It is the only coin you have, and only you can determine how it will be spent. Be careful lest you let other people spend it for you." Carl Sandburg

Creative Expression

You were a member of a rigid, restrictive, high-control environment. All the required activities in the cult and all the limits on associations and behaviours meant you could not really pursue any personal creative interests. Part of the malaise of being a Jehovah's Witness is that there is no outlet for personal or creative expression. We all have a drive to express our unique selves, be it through art, music, movement, writing, athletics, crafts, design, theatre, etc., etc. Creative expression is truly healing for the soul.

Because as a child or young adult I was never encouraged to explore creatively, I had no idea that I had a penchant or predisposition for art or design. Only since I closed my private practice and have had time to explore my creative proclivities did I discover that I had a repressed artist inside waiting for the opportunity and permission to express herself. I followed inner prompts to experiment creatively and took up photography and then noticed a desire to try to make art with some of my photographs. So I applied myself to learning how to using digital design programs. I taught myself how to digitally reconfigure my photos into 'art'. Making digital photo-art became a bit of a passion. I then had the urge to play with paint. Once started, I could not stop. What a liberating form of expression! Now large canvases of abstract, acrylic paintings spill out of every room of our house! It has been a wonderfully satisfying and therapeutic outlet for years of repressed creativity. What have you been waiting to discover, explore and express?

Now that you are free, I encourage you to make a point of engaging in some form of creative expression. Listen for any prompts from within to express yourself creatively. Whatever form of creative expression you choose will surely be deeply satisfying, a great challenge and ultimately one source of healing. Therapists often say, "*When you don't express, you depress*". They may be referring to verbal expression but creative expression also helps us not to sink into depression. Art therapists would agree. Creative expression is not a selfish indulgence. It's a human need. One you finally deserve to fulfil.

Stay In the Now

While you are working to recover from wounds of the past, while you are trying to determine how you will move ahead with your life, you don't want to dwell only in the time zones of past and future. What counts is now. In truth, there is only the now. If you really harness your mind to be in the present moment you will discover that right here, right now, everything is okay – maybe not always great – but okay. Try checking in with yourself at different moments throughout your day and ask: *Right here, right now, is everything okay?* You will be surprised, if you really stay in the moment with what is, that your answer will usually be "*Yes*".

In present moment awareness you can rest and rejuvenate. Revisiting the pain of the past and contemplating and worrying about all the unknowns of the future can be extremely stressful. Everything that really matters happens in the now. We can't change the past nor can we always accurately predict the future. We can know peace in the now.

It is my belief that real healing and real creativity only happen in the present moment. Spending all your time reliving and/or agonizing over what you've lost and what as a result you may never have, because of your relationship to the JW cult becomes counter-productive. Your tasks now are to *heal* and then to *create* a new life for yourself. Both tasks require present moment awareness. Since you want to heal the wounds from being a Jehovah's Witness and you want to develop a vision for your new life, it is essential to live in the here and now.

> *"Whatever the present moment contains, accept it as if you had chosen it. Always work with it, not against it. Make it your friend and your ally, not your enemy. This will miraculously transform your whole life."* Eckhart Tolle

> *"You must live in the present, launch yourself on every wave, find your eternity in each moment."* Henry David Thoreau

> *"Always say "yes" to the present moment. What could be more futile, more insane, than to create inner resistance to what already is? What could be more insane than to oppose life itself, which is now and always now? Surrender to what is. Say "yes" to life – and see how life suddenly starts working for you rather than against you."* Eckhart Tolle

Reclaim Your Breath

When we have lived under the control of another person or organization, when we have not been allowed to be ourselves, when so much is asked of us that we are continually stressed, when we have been misled and spiritually abused, we naturally become anxious and can even move into "fight, flight or freeze" mode. All of these emergency modalities of being affect how we breathe. When we are anxious our breathing can become shallow and shallow breathing can be indicative of a low-level state of panic. It is debilitating to live in a state of panic or semi-panic. You cannot reconnect with yourself and rebuild your life while in a state of unrecognized anxiety and when your body/mind is, in effect, starved of oxygen. Proper diaphragmatic breathing will help you relax, feel good and feel more connected to yourself. Learning to deepen, lengthen, soften and smooth out the breath can bring your entire physiology back to a place of peace. Being a Jehovah's Witness interrupted your connection with your true, authentic self and even with the free flow of your breath. You can and should take steps to remedy that now.

Fifteenth century Indian poet, Kabir tells us: *"...Student, tell me, what is God? He is the breath inside the breath."* Perhaps it is time to slow down and really breathe – breathe deeply enough that you can feel the breath within the breath. Perhaps it is time to recognize how sacred and empowering each breath is. Focusing on your breath brings you back to the present moment.

There are many different kinds of breathing exercises that can relieve stress, lower blood pressure, re-oxygenate your blood stream, help you re-establish connection to your inner self and restore calm to your nervous system. There are many good books, websites and videos that can teach you how to reconnect with your breath. Wayne Muller "Legacy of the Heart" (1993), says we can even find our true place of belonging in our breath! *"We may begin to feel our belonging in the breath -- here we may take sanctuary, here we begin to feel our place in creation. Taking refuge in each breath of life, in each beat of our heart, we find a quiet place of belonging. This refuge, this sanctuary, is neither given nor taken away by the chaotic demands of an unpredictable world. This place belongs to us, and we to it. It is where we make our home."*

Join a Healthy Group

Find a group (preferably non-denominational at first) to join, such as an exercise group, a healthy ex-JW Facebook group, a meditation group, a photography club, a biking club, etc. We become acutely aware of our human need for belonging when we are banished and/or shunned. Belonging is so important that it is one of the core human needs in psychologist Abraham Maslow's "Hierarchy of Needs". At one time the survival of the individual was inextricably linked to the tribe. Our primitive reptilian brain probably still considers belongingness a survival issue.

When we are ostracized and shunned by family and friends it can awaken some very primal feelings - feelings that can make us feel panicked. On some deep level we can feel as if our very survival is at risk. In today's world, however, that is an over-exaggeration - one that you must challenge. Yes, you will be profoundly hurt by being shunned, but you will not expire from it. Your survival on the planet is not threatened by being cut off from your family. You can help your reptilian brain calm down if you give it a bit of a sense of belonging by joining in some group activities that please and excite you - even if it is not the group of people (your family) that you are really longing for right now.

Remember, our little trick – *"relate to it, not from it"*?

> *"A part of me feels like I just cannot survive being shunned and losing my sense of belonging with my family, but I will not dwell on this irrational fear."*

> *"The old, brainwashed JW part of me resists joining groups of worldly strangers to engage in pleasant activities, but I'm going to push past that resistance and find a group that pleases me."*

By proactively reaching out to associate with others (even strangers at first) you give yourself the gift of fulfilling some belonging needs. This can help you feel better during the initial shock and pain of being ostracized. Don't necessarily wait to feel some profound interest in an activity or group. If you notice any small level of interest, get involved. Involvement often precedes interest and awakens interest.

Include Yourself

As Jehovah's Witnesses we were carefully groomed to exclude ourselves from the 'world'. We had to exclude ourselves from: worldly associations, office parties, birthday parties, gift exchanges, educational opportunities, sports activities, artistic endeavors, voting, singing of national anthems, community service, etc., etc.

It is now second nature to us to excuse and exclude ourselves from the normal activities of our friends, office colleagues, school mates, neighbors. Now that we are out of the cult and being shunned by all and sundry still in it, we may feel alone and isolated and yet still continue the pattern of excluding ourselves from enjoyable, everyday activities with others.

Even though I felt very isolated, excluded and lonely after leaving the Witnesses, I noticed that I continued the old habit of excluding myself from opportunities to join in professional or community activities. Once I noticed what I was doing I had to consciously make a point to include myself rather than automatically exclude myself. It had become my norm (from JW indoctrination) to not include myself in recreational and friend-ly-gathering-type activities. It took some conscious effort to effect the change, but it was worth it.

A couple of years after exiting the cult I took some evening courses in psychology at a local college. One evening a woman I often chatted with during class breaks suggested we go out for a drink after class to continue our discussion. Out for a drink?! With a worldly person?! It was so out of my comfort zone that my first response was to exclude myself saying that I should really just get home. She repeated the invitation and, counter to everything I felt in my body/mind, I changed my mind and said yes. I immediately doubted myself. What was I doing?! Surely I was about to sink into the debauchery the Society warned would be the result of worldly associations!

The outcome of what seemed to me like "dangerous worldly asso-ciation" was that I made a lifelong friend. Had I not been willing to go against all the old JW indoctrination and include myself by accepting her invitation, I would have missed out on a pivotal friendship in my life. This lovely woman became a cherished friend and loyal cheer-leader for my efforts to finally carve out a life for myself apart from the Jehovah's Witnesses. I, too, had the privilege of being supportive in her exceptional life journey. All because I finally stepped outside of my comfort zone and included myself.

We will remain isolated if we do not make a concerted effort to in-clude ourselves in activities around us. When someone says, "*Hey – a few of us are going out together for lunch, why don't you join us?*" why not include yourself by responding, "*I'd love to join you.*" If you walk into the workplace cafeteria and see a few people seated at a table, will you seat yourself alone at another table across the room, or will you include yourself in the group, by simply asking, "*May I join you?*" This may not be easy if, like me, you are more of an introverted person than an extrovert. But, if you don't want to remain separate, isolated and lonely, it is up to you to find ways to include yourself in life and not remain separate and aloof as was the norm as a Jehovah's Witness.

Once comfortable with this new behavior of including yourself, you can go a step further and try being the one to issue invitations to include others in enjoyable activities. Take the initiative to invite a co-worker out for a coffee. Take the initiative to organize a going-away party for a colleague at work. Invite a neighbor to go for a brisk walk with you. Go out of your way to do things where you can include others in pleasant pass-times. Most people will appreciate your thoughtfulness and will often respond in kind.

There is an active, supportive ex-JW community on Facebook with many Ex-JW Facebook groups or forums in which they gather to share experiences, ask questions, and offer help and support to one another. You will not be pushed or pressured to participate any more than you want to, but it's nice to know that there are thousands of people just like you who understand what you are going through and who will value and respect your story should you choose to share it, or questions should you choose to ask them. I hope you will consider including yourself and reap the many healing benefits available to you there.

It takes thought, attention and effort to step out of the 'separate-from-the-world', Jehovah's Witness pattern. Don't be discouraged if some of your initiatives at 'inclusion' don't always work. That's the way life is. Sometimes people are busy, pre-occupied, involved in a private discussion, in a bad mood...whatever... Don't take it personally. Sometimes you may include yourself in something you wish you hadn't. Just let a bad experience go. Learn from it and try again. Continue to try to live being inclusive, rather than exclusive as you were taught to be in the JW organization. As a free person, there are no more prohibitions on your activities, so when it feels right and/or appropriate - include yourself. Above all, don't isolate yourself. Get out. Meet people. Get involved.

The Butterfly Hug

The Butterfly Hug is a self-soothing, stress-reduction technique developed from the bilateral stimulation method of therapy known as EMDR (Eye Movement Desensitization and Reprocessing). EMDR is used by psychiatrists, psychologists and psychotherapists as a treatment for PTS and PTSD. The Butterfly Hug, a simple method for calming the self in moments of moderate anxiety, was developed when EMDR practitioners were sent to help survivors of hurricane Pauline in Mexico in 1998. They offered homeless children a way to soothe themselves and minimize their emotional pain.

The premise is that with alternating taps on each side of the body, we stimulate the two hemispheres of the brain. This bilateral stimulation of the brain seems to help any stuck or looping feelings to move with more ease between both hemispheres and benefit from whole-brain reprocessing rather than remaining lodged firing and re-firing repeatedly in one part of the brain.

Of course, this premise is very difficult to test and prove but that is the current working theory for why the treatment works. However it works, it is a benign activity designed to comfort and calm any traumatized person. Tons of anecdotal feedback from around the world does confirm its efficacy. It is a wonderful little tool to have in your private healing toolkit! We don't have to find ourselves in the midst of a natural catastrophe or be a victim of war to use it. Use it anytime you feel you need a little help to manage distress, anxiety or depression. Here are the simple instructions:

Sit as comfortably as possible and take a few deep breaths. Notice what you are feeling (anxiety, sadness, loneliness, fear) without trying to change the feeling or avoid it. Just be present to whatever your body/mind is experiencing. Place your right hand on your left shoulder and your left hand on your right shoulder. This means that your arms are crossed across your chest giving you the feeling of hugging yourself – hence the name Hug. The taps feel like butterfly wings – hence the name Butterfly.

With your hands alternating, gently tap your shoulders with your hands - like fluttering butterfly wings. It is important to alternate the taps. Tap on your left shoulder. Then tap on your right shoulder. You can decide on the speed you want to tap, just make sure that you are alternating the taps.

Continue the tapping for approximately a minute. Make sure you are breathing normally while you are doing the alternating taps. Continue to be present to whatever is happening in your mind, body or emotions without judging, changing or avoiding anything. After a minute or so of tapping stop and take a deep cleansing breath. Notice whether your level of stress or anxiety has diminished. You can do as many sets of taps as you wish.

This EMDR Butterfly Hug is a self-soothing method you can use whenever you feel moderately anxious or distressed. Not every technique works for every person, but this technique has proved to be very effective and was used with both children and adults in Nicaragua, Mexico and Kosovo refugee camps (Shapiro, 2001, p. 284). The Butterfly Hug has become standard practice for EMDR clinicians working with the Humanitarian Assistance Program across the globe. There are probably some YouTube videos that demonstrate the technique, if you would like to see it in action before you try it.

You could also do a Google search for the slightly more complicated "Havening" technique developed by Ronald A. Ruden (When the Past is Always Present, 2010). Havening seems to have been developed using these same bilateral stimulation principles from EMDR. Ruden uses stroking of the arms in combination with bilateral eye movements.

If you find yourself feeling anxious in public and do not want to do the Butterfly Hug for all and sundry to see, you can modify it (leave out the hug part) by putting your hands on or beside each leg and making little alternating taps with one or two fingers of each hand. Tap on one leg, then on the other leg - for several seconds. Or, cross your arms in the way most of us do now and then, and do alternating taps with your thumbs on the under part of your arms. These easy variations will still help you balance the input of both sides of your brain and calm your anxiety without being noticed in a public setting.

Now you have probably figured out why you feel so good after a walk or a jog. It is not just the fresh air pumping into your lungs and the cardio-vascular workout. When you walk you are using one leg, then the other – swinging one arm then the other. You are giving your brain some bilateral stimulation which helps you move into a whole-brain modality of thinking. When you feel down go outside for a brisk walk.

With the bilateral movements of walking you are helping yourself in a variety of ways, including a variation of a bilateral stimulation of your brain hemispheres – a free mini-EMDR treatment that you can give yourself!

Look Up

Try this: When feeling sad or blue, literally LOOK UP. The unconscious knowing of the relevance and benefits of this advice is heard in the everyday expression, *"Things are looking up."* Perhaps you have noticed that someone who is crying may try to stop the crying by rolling their eyeballs upwards. It seems to be an automatic response. This "looking up" is done with only the eye balls, not the head. Roll your eyes (not your head) up, while focusing on something above you. Then ... try to feel depressed. Go ahead... Try to feel depressed while you look up with your eyes in that position. You can't. Now, try the opposite. Look down, let your shoulders slump, drop your head and cast your eyes down toward your navel. You cannot help but feel your mood slump too. Interesting isn't it? Upward eye movements seem to make it difficult to feel depressed, even when we are!

So the lesson is, when feeling depressed or sad move your eyes upward in their socket. Look up. Look up at the tops of buildings as you walk down the street. (Don't do this crossing the street or in crowds!) Look up at the tops of trees. Look up at the clouds. Look up at the ceiling in your home. It is almost impossible to feel sadness when your eyes are in that upward position. I know you can't walk around this way all the time and you have to look out for your safety, but you can use this technique for a few moments of relief when you feel sadness, longing or despair creeping up on you.

"...remember to look up at the stars and not down at your feet." Stephen Hawking

Let Nature Mother You

There's a reason that we sometimes bestow nature with the adjective "Mother". A stroll by the ocean, a walk in the woods, a night under the stars, a hike up a mountain, an afternoon sitting beside a mountain stream – any human connection with nature's offerings – delivers a restorative, calming influence. Like D.W. Winnicott's description of a good mother, nature welcomes us, holds us, does not interfere with us, does not abandon us, and above all, never judges us. If you are being shunned you need to reinforce your connection with nature as frequently as possible. Discover how nature can serve as a loving holding environment for you. If you are cut off from your home and family let Mother Nature be your home. Visit Mother Nature often, she is always available to receive you. Soak up all the healing energy she has to offer.

Silence, Stillness, Solitude

Give yourself the gift of quiet moments, free of ideology, expectations, fears, regrets, worries, etc. Moments of simply being silent and still. Moments of solitude where you can experience the beauty of *simply being* without interference or interruption. I wish I had discovered the following sets of wise words encouraging silence, stillness and solitude after I exited the JW cult. They would have been a source of balm to my agitated, nervous, confused self.

> *"The capacity to be alone with no visible means of support is one of the most important signs of maturity in emotional development."* D.W. Winnicott

> *"There is nothing in all creation so like God as stillness."* Meister Eckhart

> *"Anything you want to ask a teacher, ask yourself, and wait for the answer in silence."* Byron Katie

Sometimes when you try to enjoy some solitude, silence and stillness you may find that intrusive thoughts keep rushing in, creating an inner disturbance. This is where learning the technique of mindfulness or learning how to meditate can be of help. There are many great instructional videos online that can help you learn these peaceful ways of being. You can find many websites or videos on the web for beginners wanting to learn the basics of mindfulness or meditation.

I highly recommend the website of teacher Tara Brach (tarabrach.com). She has a page on her site where she offers the free download of a booklet on *"How to Meditate"*. Tara Brach is a Ph.D. in psychology as well as a meditation instructor. There are many of Dr. Brach's lectures on her YouTube channel. Her lectures are really worth listening to if you are interested in living an awakened, present, peaceful life.

Meditation is a wonderful tool to invoke a mindful presence that awakens one to the underlying peaceful nature of both inner and outer reality. As said, I wish someone had pointed me to the healing effects possible via a mindful approach to life and via meditation when I first left the JW movement.

I now make a point of inserting many spontaneous meditative moments into all of my days. After practicing meditation and mindfulness over a period of time you will find that it becomes a way of being and that you can easily shift from a concentrated focus on a situation or project into a transcendent state of pure, peaceful awareness with immediacy and ease. ("Transcendent" is not some occult or weird term, by the way. Transcendent only means you have learned to transcend (rise above) your egoic mind, its incessant thinking, its preoccupations and its many self-absorbed states.)

"Not to be able to stop thinking is a dreadful affliction, but we don't realize this because almost everyone is suffering from it, so it is considered normal. This incessant mental noise prevents you from finding that realm of inner stillness that is inseparable from Being." Eckhart Tolle

"One must learn an inner solitude, wherever one may be." Meister Eckhart

CHAPTER 18

Adult Development
Pre-Empted By Indoctrination

When a religious group claims:

- to have a direct line to *the* truth
- to be directed by God Almighty to interpret his written word
- to have absolute knowledge of how humanity's future will unfold
- to know that "millions now living will never die"
- to know that God will destroy wicked non-believers at Armageddon
- to know exactly what you have to do in order to survive Armageddon and live forever
- you must sacrifice all personal desires and goals and devote yourself to preaching God's good news of the kingdom
- you must limit your associations and activities to ones prescribed for you by them

then there are many psycho/social developmental tasks of childhood and adulthood that remain unaddressed for the individuals trapped in such deluded indoctrination.

Erik Erikson, psychologist and psychoanalyst developed an eight stage theory showing the normal phases of development through which every healthy human should pass, from infancy to late adulthood. In each of the eight stages humans are confronted with crises or challenges that need to be negotiated in order not to be left with deficits in normal development, which ultimately affects psychological and social growth and maturity. Being in the JW cult, means you may not have been free to confront these psychosocial challenges and thus were not able to claim the adult identity, autonomy, and competencies as easily as you might have done.

Erikson's Eight Stage Theory of PsychoSocial Development

	AGE	VIRTUES	PSYCHOSOCIAL CRISIS	SIGNIFICANT RELATIONSHIP	EXISTENTIAL QUESTION	EXAMPLES
1.	0-2 years	Hopes	Basic Trust vs. Mistrust	Mother	Can I trust the world?	Feeding, Abandonment
2.	2-4 years	Will	Autonomy vs. Shame and Doubt	Parents	Is it OK to be me?	Toilet Training Clothing Self
3.	4-5 years	Purpose	Initiative vs. Guilt	Family	Is it OK for me to Do, Move, Act?	Exploring, Using Tools Making art
4.	5-12 years	Competence	Industry vs. Inferiority	Neighbors, School	Can I Make it in a world of people and things?	School Sports
5.	13-19 years	Fidelity	Identity vs. Role Confusion	Peers, Role Models	Who am I? What can I be?	Social Relationships
6.	20-24 years	Love	Intimacy vs. Isolation	Friends, Partners	Can I love?	Romantic Relationships
7.	25-64 years	Care	Generativity vs. Stagnation	Household, Workmates	Can I make my life count?	Work, Parenthood
8.	65- death	Wisdom	Ego Integrity vs. Despair	Mankind, My Kind	Is it OK to have been me?	Reflections on Life

Erik Erikson's Eight Stage Theory of Psychosocial Development

As you look at the above chart, you may see that many of the developmental tasks of life are aborted, pre-empted or denied to members of the Jehovah's Witnesses cult. For example, as a Jehovah's Witness were you able to:

- explore
- be creative
- participate in sports
- develop a variety of social relationships
- take initiative
- explore romantic relationships before marriage
- educate yourself
- develop a variety of competencies

- select a purpose for your life that was your own
- choose a satisfying way to support yourself
- learn to make your way comfortably in the world
- make your life count for something
- find time to reflect upon your life in your way
- develop your own wisdom to share with the next generation

As one of Jehovah's Witnesses, I was not able to explore, participate, choose, be creative, or educate myself. If you take some time to look at Erikson's chart, you can determine if you think you were able to successfully negotiate each developmental stage up to your present age, while a member of the JW organization.

Ask yourself the questions that go with the challenge of each stage, under the heading "*Existential Questions*". If you were raised in a strict cult such as the Jehovah's Witnesses, you will probably find that your answer to most of the questions will be "*No*" or "*I don't know*". Whereas an adult who successfully negotiates these psychosocial stages free from cult, religious, parental interference would most likely answer "*Yes*".

Why would this be? Because when you find yourself in an organization that exercises rigid control over behavior, thought and access to information, that has all the rules and answers for everything, that tells you how to run your life, that discourages reflection, introspection and the asking of questions, that discourages exploration and social interactions, then the Erikson developmental challenges and tasks, the learning from completing the tasks, the growth possible, are all pre-empted - left undone.

Being one of Jehovah's Witnesses prevents one from addressing many of these normal psychosocial stages of development. Normal developmental maturation may be somewhat arrested. The JW organization's control over the mind, plus all the control over the activities of its followers interfere with the developmental evolution of these psychological and social stages of life. This could account for our willingness to be led, to not question, to not make our own decisions, to not make waves, and even to not leave. The JW cult keeps us, to a degree, in a servile child-like mentality, all the more ready to accept their indoctrination and influence.

Eric Hoffer, in his seminal book, "The True Believer" describes this phenomenon as one common to all mass movements, *"To the frustrated, freedom from responsibility is more attractive than freedom from restraint. They are eager to barter their independence for relief from the burdens of willing, deciding and being responsible for inevitable failure. They willingly abdicate the directing of their lives to those who want to plan, command and shoulder all responsibility."* p. 118

Now if you were raised as a Jehovah's Witness you did not necessarily "barter" away your independence or "abdicate" away your authority over your life. Rather it was more likely done to you. As Jehovah's Witnesses we were literally seduced, conned and brainwashed. From a distance it is easy to see the initial attraction to a group that provides all the answers and makes all the decisions...

But what does this mean for you if you exit the organization? It means that now out of the religion you finally stand alone and free, in the middle of this big, beautiful, complex world, feeling slightly ill-equipped and even insecure. Why? Because you have been denied the right to develop fully as an adult, assuming adult independence and shouldering responsibility for your future. Is all lost? Certainly not. But there is a little catching up for you to do developmentally especially in the areas of "will", "purpose" and perhaps "competence", on Erikson's chart.

A lot of this catching up will happen automatically as you move forward with life, free from the interference of a self-serving, controlling outside authority. But you need to know that for a time you may feel slightly ill-prepared to fashion your new life. One of the good results of leaving the organization is that you will be forced now to grow into who you were meant to be before they interfered in your natural development.

When an organization has you believing that you are to do nothing that they have not sanctioned for you, you stop exploring. There is no need to explore, discover, think, evaluate or challenge yourself with new activities. Your autonomy, your true self is squashed when you are told what to believe, what to do, how to do it. Your capacity to "will" or act on your own behalf is not encouraged or exercised. You have been infantilized, encouraged to continue in the 'magical thinking' stage of childhood, accepting (on the surface) all pronouncements for your life from a harsh, parental substitute known as the governing body.

In fact, some of you may even feel some shame or doubt when you begin to exercise your free will by making your own choices and decisions. For example, did or do you experience doubt and uncertainty when you consider reading a book by someone who stopped believing in what the Jehovah's Witnesses teach? Are you feeling a bit guilty now as you exercise your will to read a book critical of JW.ORG and that makes suggestions as to how you can recover from the spiritual and psychological abuses of the organization?

The leadership of the JW cult has worked hard at programming this very reaction into you because they are afraid you may find out about all their deceptions and leave. Remember, there is another part of you trying to push past all that programming and learn if what you have been following is really the truth. If you are reading this book your strength to push past the first voice of old programming and listen to your true inner voice is evident!

When you are denied the right to exercise your own *initiative*, to ask questions, to determine your own *purpose* in life, to initiate your own plans and see them through to completion, you never have the pleasure or experience of feeling *free* and *independent*. Nor do you develop the full capacity of *courage* that comes with completing independent initiatives.

When you are told everything you supposedly need to know by some higher executive authority you lose touch with your own needs, preferences, desires, life purpose and inner authority. If some needs and/or desires do break through into consciousness you will probably feel some neurotic guilt. And, of course, you will feel even more neurotic guilt if you dare to act upon your desires in contravention of their commands. We have already addressed the issue of neurotic guilt in a previous chapter.

The governing body of Jehovah's Witnesses limit your access to the information that is available to the rest of the world. They try to crush your curiosity. They deny you the right to ask questions and tell you they will provide all the spiritual food you will ever need. You are often told to "*wait on Jehovah to provide the answers in due time*". You are patronized and worse yet, discouraged from using your innate critical thinking skills and even your right to will (act) on your own behalf. This is psychological abuse.

When you live in a restrictive, closed environment such as the one created by the JW organization, the only way to experience a feeling of *competence* is by being obedient to their prescriptions for your life and following all their rules. Rank and file Jehovah's Witnesses feel good about themselves when following the governing body's instructions. They have been trained to feel that when you are a dutiful Jehovah's Witness, you are competent, good and pleasing to Almighty God. You are discouraged from expanding any of your real, innate competencies because they tell you that participation in sports, higher education, artistic endeavors, social exchanges, etc., will pull you away from God's assignments and expose you to bad associations. This, too, is psychological abuse.

Having a lid put on your ability to explore talents, friendships and competencies can diminish your motivation, independence and *self-confidence*. You end up feeling a bit inferior to others you see who are free to try out new things. Of course, truth be told, you have been groomed to not be aware of your own talents, to be dependent, to not act with any autonomy as this serves the needs of the controlling organization to have you be pliable to their will. This is what cults do to their members and it is abusive.

We have had a little glimpse into some of what has been denied you by being under the control of the Watchtower Bible & Tract Society. But not to worry, with a little time, with some gentle awareness you will revisit these areas and negotiate these stages of development. With some conscious effort, you will reclaim all the competencies that may have been delayed, and more! As a human being you are wired to develop into a free-thinking, autonomous adult and now that you are able to live freely, you will.

So ... if you recently exited the Watchtower organization expect to grapple, for a bit, with occasional feelings of doubt, guilt or even inferiority. This is normal for any human being who has been held psychologically captive and brainwashed in a cult. It does not mean there is something wrong with you, nor does it mean you made the wrong decision by leaving. Keep calm and carry on, as they say. During the process of living as a free agent you will develop the inner authority, competence and confidence you need.

Go back briefly to the column "Existential Questions" in the Erikson chart. I have just written about the second, third and fourth psychosocial challenges and recommend that you take the existential questions for those three stages and use the information there to your advantage. Here's how: remember you are doing some cult 'deprogramming' and developmental work for yourself. So for example, take the third question, *"Is it okay for me to do, move and act?"* Ask it of yourself, and answer *"YES!"* with enthusiasm!

If you notice some part of you really wants to answer "no", just allow that thought to be there and continue to answer in the affirmative anyway. This is the time to use the hackneyed expression "fake it 'til you make it". Sometimes expressions like that are overused for a reason - they work!

Is it okay for me to DO? YES!
Is it okay for me to MOVE? YES!
Is it okay for me to ACT? YES!

If I had known about having missed out on negotiating these psycho-social developmental stages when I exited from the Jehovah's Witnesses, I would have better understood the need to affirm on a daily basis my ability to do, move and act until I had integrated these abilities as my own. I would have shouted in my own mind (and maybe from the rooftops), over and over again:

- It's okay to be autonomous and independent!
- It's okay to think my own thoughts!
- It's okay to make my own choices!
- It's okay to change my mind!
- It's okay to say, "No"!
- It's okay to say, "Yes!"
- It's okay to enjoy associations with other humans on planet earth!
- I refuse to doubt, shame or guilt myself!
- I refuse to ignore my valid questions and always "wait on Jehovah" for the answers.
- I will do my own research and educate myself!

Don't allow yourself to feel silly or self-conscious as you repeat or write the above statements. You must replace years of programming with new thoughts that will affirm your right to be you, your right to make your own decisions, your right to develop fully as a free, autonomous adult. If you continue to repeat the statements with enthusiasm and belief, your body/

mind will begin to accept them as now being true for you. The goal is that these new self-affirming beliefs will then start to be reflected in your life.

"*As a single footstep will not make a path on the earth, so a single thought will not make a pathway in the mind. To make a deep physical path, we walk again and again. To make a deep mental path, we must think over and over the kind of thoughts we wish to dominate our lives.*" Henry David Thoreau

With Erikson's Stages of Psychosocial Development you have seen some of the necessary maturation process that was temporarily denied you by being in the controlling Jehovah's Witnesses cult. It seems so obvious now how it serves the needs of the JW governing body to inhibit our ability to will for ourselves, to think for ourselves, and to be independent. But now out of the cult we will catch up in our psycho-social development and exercise our competence and agency on our own behalf.

CHAPTER 19

Ultimate Concerns of Facing Life, Free

There are core, fundamental issues that every human being has to address. These issues are not always easy to confront especially if you have been confined, shut off and sheltered in a cult. Membership in the Jehovah's Witness cult with their strict beliefs and rigid controls can actually serve as a maladaptive means to escape wrestling with some of the basic realities of life, also known as, **the existential givens of life**. An existential given is a reality that every human will have to deal with at one time or another throughout their lifetime. It's a 'given' that you will have to confront them!

The Jehovah's Witness organization, can serve for some, as a shelter (albeit a temporary and controlling one) from some of these harsh realities (givens) of existence. Psychoanalyst James Hollis, asks: *"Where do you refuse to grow up, wait for certainty of vision before choosing, hope for solutions to emerge fully formed, expect rescue, or wait for a guru to make sense of it all for you?"* ("On This Journey We Call Our Life", p.45)

Let's take a look at what philosophers and psychologists identify as the main ultimate concerns (existential realities or givens) with which every human must grapple sooner or later, and that Jehovah's Witnesses generally avoid:

Existential Reality of Death: *I am mortal. This body of mine will die.* With this existential given, I must deal with my human limitations, with the fact that I am not exempt from what will happen to everyone else (the death of the body). Given the fact I am not exempt from the reality of death, I am, therefore, not special.

Existential Realities of Freedom and Responsibility: *I am free to choose. I must exercise my will on my behalf.* With this existential given I must grapple with my own agency in the world, and while I have often said I want to be free, I know I may be unconsciously afraid of the responsibilities that come with that desired freedom.

Existential Reality of Basic Aloneness: *No matter who surrounds me I am basically alone.* With this existential given I am forced to realize that no one can make key decisions for me - the task is mine alone. Ultimately, no matter who surrounds me, only I can live my life and experience my joys, my pain, my illnesses, my death. I alone must decide how connected or disconnected I will be to others throughout my lifetime, and even more importantly how connected or disconnected I will be to my inner self.

Existential Reality of Meaninglessness: *Only I can make my life meaningful by doing things that provide meaning for me.* With this existential concern I am forced to realize that if I allow someone else to decide what is meaningful for me, I will most likely experience deep meaninglessness and despair at the end of my days. (One does not necessarily decide on meaning. Meaning comes as a result of a full, active engagement with life.)

By espousing the beliefs of the Watchtower Bible & Tract Society some followers discover (more on an unconscious level than a conscious one) that they can escape the anxiety of struggling with the above fundamental realities of existence. Unfortunately, such an illusory, temporary escape inhibits growth and, therefore, maturity.

For a Jehovah's Witness still caught up in the cult, their thoughts about the above givens of existence might sound like this:

A JW take on the existential reality of Death: *As a JW I am promised everlasting life. I will not die if I am obedient. I am, therefore, exempt from having to come to terms with a limited life. I have the truth. That, and being exempt from death, makes me special.*

A JW take on the existential realities of Freedom and Responsibility:
As a JW I do not have to worry about freedom or the responsibilities freedom brings. I have turned over my ability to decide and act to JW.ORG. I do not have to risk acting on my own and failing. I don't have to assume the responsibilities of being free in this world. I trust in Jehovah and his organization to guide me. As a JW I simply have to follow and obey. It is the JW truth that sets me free.

A JW take on the existential reality of Isolation: *As a JW I am never really alone. Jehovah is always with me guiding my life. I also have the loving "Faithful & Discreet Slave" who provide me with spiritual food and direction, and I lean on them. They dispense God's truth and God's new light when the 'truth' proves fleeting. I am always surrounded by, welcomed by, and busy with other devotees and really never have to experience my basic aloneness. It is more important for me to connect with Jehovah, his truth and his organization than to selfishly know and connect with myself.*

A JW take on the existential reality of Meaning: *As a JW I will never know meaninglessness. I am a servant of Almighty God and have been assigned the important task of warning the world, through the Kingdom preaching work, that He will soon destroy the wicked. What could be more meaningful than saving people from annihilation at Armageddon? What could be more meaningful than serving Jehovah throughout eternity? I do not have to grapple with creating anything meaningful of my own, on my own. My association with Jehovah's Witnesses provides all the meaning I need ... I think.*

Sobering isn't it? Eric Hoffer, way back in 1951 described this very tendency of mass movements to shelter their adherents from the realities of life and thereby exercise absolute control over them, "*All active mass movements strive ...* **to interpose a fact-proof screen between the faithful and the realities of the world**. *They do this by claiming that the ultimate and absolute truth is already embodied in their doctrine and that there is no truth nor certitude outside it.*"(The True Believer, p. 79) (Bold mine.)

Hoffer's description is, all these years later, still true - certainly of the Jehovah's Witness cult. While the Watchtower Society may claim to have the "absolute truth", eventually we each have to ask ourselves if we have used the cushion of the JW version of truth to shelter us from confronting the essential concerns of being human on planet Earth … and, at what cost?

The thing is the Society can seem to offer shelter from harsh realities but ultimately the process of life intercedes and demands that we confront these issues on our own whether inside of or outside of a cult. When we don't know about them, and don't address them, these realities visit us anyway and we can find ourselves terribly unprepared and, therefore exceedingly anxious.

Jungian analyst and author, James Hollis, asks: *"Where am I asking others to take responsibility for my life? Let's face it - we would all love to be taken care of. We all are recovering children who project the dynamics of the intrapsychic parent onto an institution, an ideology …Growing up is ever more difficult because it requires letting go of old expectations of rescue and redemption. We are it; this is it; this is as good as it gets, and we better deal with it."* (Creating A Life, p. 121) I encourage you to read this Hollis quotation a second time! *"This is it"* and there is no time to waste! Hollis' many books can really help one come to terms with how to live an authentic, mature, meaningful life.

I often wonder about loyal JWs from the last century (such as my mother) who sheltered in and worked so hard for the JW organization. They expected to see the fulfillment of all the prophecies, as interpreted by and promised to them for decades by the Society. They had been promised rescue, redemption and eternal life in paradise! They expected to be taken care of by Jehovah and his organization forever. How terrifying it must have been to be old and frail and have to confront not only profound disappointment but also the realities of life they believed they would not have to confront: death, aloneness, responsibility and meaninglessness.

Will today's Jehovah's Witnesses also lay on their death bed realizing they will probably not survive Armageddon? Will they, too, be dismayed to discover they may not number among those who will never die? Can they count on a resurrection to a paradise earth? Is the resurrection but a consoling myth? Will they slowly realize they have been misled and used? Will they wonder if they sacrificed their lives for an illusion of truth? Will they realize that they gave up their freedom, were lied to, and the perpetrators of the lies don't care and take no responsibility?

The perpetrators of the lies will not step up and face these harsh realities for them – the rank and file must do it alone. The Governing Body is too busy trying to captivate and control the next generation of servants. Will today's JWs realize that they perhaps led others (their precious children among them) to compromise their freedom and personal agency too? If the end keeps being delayed, ad infinitum, was it all a hoax? Did their spiritual life ever really have any worthy purpose? At what cost did they isolate themselves from life, the world, and most importantly from themselves? Have they aligned themselves to something that was, in the end, a pitiful delusion?

Imagine the existential anxiety, dread and desolation loyal devotees have had to, and will have to, face at the end of their years of ultimately futile service to the JW organization. It breaks my heart to think of their inevitable disappointment and despair.

If you are exiting the cult, or have already done so, the above-mentioned existential concerns will be waiting to be addressed. You will no longer be temporarily cushioned and comforted by Watchtower's false promises and deluded thinking. This may account for some of the fear, anxiety and depression that we experience when we leave the cult. It is called "existential angst". It is part of being human to experience existential angst. It takes time to deal with the existential realities of life. It requires that we be confronted with each of the ultimate concerns of life: death, aloneness, freedom, responsibility and meaning.

Fortunately we are not usually confronted by the existential givens all at once. We come to terms with these realities by participating in life as fully as we can and on an unconscious level our psyche is always working at adapting to these deep, human concerns. Much of the work of coming to terms with the realities of life is actually done for us at an unconscious level. When these concerns bubble up to consciousness, as they will throughout any life, there are ways to support ourselves through the conscious encounter. Namely: *acceptance and presence*. The good thing is that after each brush with an existential reality we emerge (whether we are consciously aware or not) as a stronger, wiser, more authentic human being.

Having walked away from the cushion of JW delusions against the realities of life (which kept us child-like and susceptible to their designs) it behooves one to take some time to think and reflect about these realities (mainly the first three as we address the fourth more through our actions than our reflections). They require some conscious introspection. We need to stop now and then to reflect, to be with what is, and to acknowledge the realities of life.

Coming to terms with the existential givens of life is something that is usually done over a lifetime but we who were members of the Jehovah's Witness religion, having thought we had been given all 'the answers', having believed we had 'the truth' and that we were therefore special and exempt, have a little catching up to do. Just knowing what you are dealing with helps. Reading what you have just read should actually be a great help. If you experience existential anxiety while embarking on your new life and facing the realities of existence you could mistakenly attribute the anxiety to other things. You could think, *"If I'm experiencing this much anxiety since leaving the Witnesses, maybe it indicates I made a mistake. Maybe this discomfort or angst means I should return to the JW organization even if it is deluded and abusive."*

No, it does not mean you have made a mistake and should go back. It simply means you are no longer living a life of delusion. You are fully alive, facing reality and confronting the same concerns that billions of humans before you have had to confront. You are no longer cushioned from reality by JW lies.

You have hopefully given up the belief in an ultimate rescuer. You have given up the belief that you are special, uniquely blessed and therefore exempt. You realize that you are not in possession of THE truth. You are stepping up to life as an adult, not remaining an infantilized dependent needing the direction of a few 'truth-holding' Governing Body members. You are coming to terms with the fact that there is no "ultimate rescuer". You are embracing a life of reality, uncertainty and incredible possibility. It seems we have the choice to embrace uncertainty and be revitalized by it or embrace a false sense of safety and ultimately be dulled and depressed by it. It helps to have this understanding as you embark on your new, free life.

Actually with the very act of leaving the cult you are, to a degree, confronting each of the four existential concerns. You have taken the *responsibility* to claim your right to *freedom* and you now stand *alone* ready to make *meaning* in your life as you define it, and at the same time you allow the knowledge of your body's *mortality* to heighten appreciation for every precious, reclaimed moment of life.

- Now out, you have to confront the fact that you are mortal - you will not survive some imaginary, ever-imminent 'War of The Worlds' and live forever in some serene paradise. *But you will live free in the eternal now and appreciate your precious life more than ever!*
- Now out, you have to confront the fact that with the freedom gained you have the responsibility to choose, decide and act for yourself. You are no longer a sheltered, obedient servant. You finally get to create and direct your life on your own. *Perhaps a little scary at first, but what a trip! Try to feel empowered rather than scared.*
- Now out, you have to confront that you are ultimately alone and with the opening in your life created by exiting the JW organization you have the internal space and freedom to get to know yourself. Finally you will discover who you always can rely on when feeling alone - YOU! You can learn to rely on your true self and not always look for an external parental substitute to guide you. *What a long-overdue opportunity to establish and solidify the most precious, reliable relationship of all – the one with your true self!*
- Now out, you have the privilege of experimenting with time, space and life to discover what matters to you and how you will engage with life to bring meaning to yourself and those around you. You will decide what is significant for you. You can finally become fully involved with, and engaged with, real life. You can use your one and only life to create YOUR life's masterpiece! *At last!*

Don't worry about having to actively and consciously wrestle these realities of life to the ground all at once, all the time. As mentioned earlier, your unconscious does a great deal of the 'coming to terms' work for you. Sometimes a little anxiety signals the conscious self that the unconscious is confronting one of life's ultimate concerns. Any anxiety you experience facing the realities of existence can then be used consciously as a guide to a more authentic life. If you notice yourself experiencing some anxiety, you can ask yourself:

"What existential reality is life asking me to face, that I may be avoiding?"

"What existential reality or concern do I need to address now?"

"When I experience the uncertainty of real life and the accompanying anxiety, what can I do instead of just hoping it will go away?"

Then as authentically as you can, calmly examine your circumstances and be truthful with yourself about what you are facing and what options are open to you. Ask yourself *"What action would most benefit me now?"* Sit and listen for the answer your psyche offers up. Living authentically like this will increase your awareness, your vitality, your creativity and your general life satisfaction.

Remember, **leaving a cult is a huge transition - an existential transition - and some accompanying anxiety is to be expected**. The exciting thing is that confronting the realities of existence will make you a more mature, authentic, psychologically aware human being than the shallow, one-dimensional level of development you could attain operating from the delusions of the Watchtower teachings. Nobody deals with these existential givens all the time. Most of the time we suppress knowledge of them in order to get on with our daily life. A degree of daily suppression is appropriate. But now and then, when these realities come to the surface, you will know what is happening and look at it as an opportunity to further grow into maturity and authenticity with strength, understanding, dignity and integrity. By so doing, you will not struggle with delusions, disappointments, meaninglessness, angst and depression on your deathbed like other poor folks we know and still love.

CHAPTER 20

The Power of Self-Love & Self-Acceptance

Self-acceptance and self-love are ultimately the most important healing gifts you can give to yourself. It is shocking to realize how few of us truly accept and love ourselves. It seems that Western culture, and certainly membership in a controlling, fundamentalist cult, fosters much self-disdain even self-hatred. At a conference in the West, the Dalai Lama was asked by a Westerner what he thought of self-hatred. Even though he speaks English he requested a translation of the question. After hearing the question in his own language he still did not seem to understand it. Finally he turned to the questioner and said, "*Self-hatred? What is that?*" Imagine! Tibetans do not even understand the concept of self-hatred and yet it is so pervasive in Western culture. If you think you may have any such feelings, your work is to learn to replace them with self-compassion. Tara Brach, says, "*Feeling compassion for ourselves in no way releases us from responsibility for our actions. Rather, it releases us from the self-hatred that prevents us from responding to our life with clarity and balance.*"

Many therapists believe that it is not the particular school of therapy, not the techniques, the methods, the interpretations, the topics of conversation, the release of pent-up emotion, etc. that do the main work of healing in therapy. Rather, they hypothesize, it is the actual relationship of the client with the therapist. It is the therapist offering presence, acceptance and unconditional positive regard throughout the course of therapy that seems to truly effect the healing. When a psychotherapist offers unconditional acceptance and non-judgmental presence it acts as a mirror for the client and they see themselves, perhaps for the first time, as good enough, as likeable, lovable and worthy. Once they internalize and own that unconditional acceptance of self, they can feel ready to embrace life with all its challenges and make the life changes they need to make. What can we learn from that? Don't wait for a therapist to offer you unconditional acceptance. Learn to offer unconditional love and acceptance to yourself now. You can pay a therapist to model unconditional acceptance for you or you can begin now to give it to yourself – for free!

The JW governing body has trained the elders and JW rank and file to look down on anyone who is disfellowshipped or who chooses to leave the group. They let us know in no uncertain terms that we are 'bad' in their eyes and in the eyes of Jehovah. It is hard to walk away from that cult without still hearing their condemnations and death threats ringing in our ears. Some Watchtower articles even encourage their membership to loathe JW defectors. Due to this, many of us leave feeling bad about ourselves, internalizing their hatred of us and even ending up consciously or unconsciously hating ourselves. Only we can change or undo this.

No one comes into the world feeling self-hate. It is something put upon us by a toxic environment and unfortunately, often it sticks. Self-hatred is usually accompanied by shame. Unconscious self-hatred can manifest as conscious depression. **Know you are not hateful. Know you are not shameful.** Those labels are not and were never true and you must work to relinquish them. Those false labels belong to the ones who speak them. They do not belong to us. They were put upon us and are not ours. It is our job to release any self-hate, self-recriminations, self-contempt and shame. It is our job to learn to love and accept our self and our life again. Tara Brach adds, "*With an undefended heart, we can fall in love with life over and over every day. We can become children of wonder, grateful to be walking on earth, grateful to belong with each other and to all of creation. We can find our true refuge in every moment, in every breath.*" (True Refuge, 2013)

If you truly want to heal from spiritual abuse the task for you is to unconditionally love and accept yourself. This, my friend is the most important and most powerful thing I can share with you. If I could distill all of what I've learned from the study of psychology, my experience as a therapist, and an on-going flirtation with Eastern philosophy into one summary sentence, it would simply be: **Love and accept yourself.** Everything else seems to fall into place from there. You don't have to go anywhere or pay anything to love and accept yourself. It's an inside job. Step up and accept yourself unconditionally now.

Listen to how Carl Rogers, the founder of the humanist, person-centered approach to therapy, thought about himself with all his normal, human frailties and imperfections: *"I have come to prize each emerging facet of my experience, of myself. I would like to treasure the feelings of anger and tenderness and shame and hurt and love and anxiety and giving and fear – all the positive and negative reactions that crop up. I would like to treasure the ideas that emerge – foolish, creative, bizarre, sound, trivial – all part of me. I like the behavioral impulses – appropriate, crazy, achievement-oriented, sexual, murderous. I want to accept all of these feelings, ideas, and impulses as an enriching part of me. I don't expect to act on all of them, but when I accept them all, I can be more real; my behavior, therefore, will be much more appropriate to the immediate situation."* Carl R. Rogers, (A Way of Being, 1995)

While being condemned by your former religion, while being shunned and thereby shamed by your family and former spiritual brothers and sisters, it is hard to maintain a loving sense of positive self-regard. It is so easy to follow suit and come down hard on one's self. A lack of positive self-regard can precipitate depression so it is imperative that you work at loving and accepting yourself through all of, and in spite of, the negative effects that result from having been a member of a cult.

This does not mean you accept all and any bad behavior from yourself, however. It means that you try to understand where the 'bad' behavior comes from. Although you don't accept errant behavior you totally accept the person (yourself) who got caught up in it. If you catch yourself in some less than admirable behavior, help yourself by saying something like, *"I don't want to do such a thing again. How will I do things differently the next time I find myself in such a circumstance?"* Answer filling in the behavior you would prefer to see - all the while loving the sweet, imperfect, evolving self that you are.

Remember our dis-identification technique? You can use it here too. *Relate to* any foibles or weaknesses you discover, *not from* them. Know they are there, but as Rogers suggests, view them as wonderfully curious, quirky, enriching *parts* of yourself, not your whole self. Remember you do not have to act from less than admirable parts of yourself. Simply acknowledge that they are there (relate to) but act from your centered adult self.

Buddhist teacher Stephen Levine tells us to love ourselves as if we were our only child. What a tender, compassionate thought! Would you judge and criticize a hurt, abused, shamed, shunned and discarded child? No you would pull him up on your knee and surround him with your arms and your love. Love yourself as if you were your only child ... now.

How does one love them self as if they were their only child? It might sound something like this: *"There, there Sweetheart...I know you are feeling sad and lonely. I totally understand. Don't worry, I'm here with you and I won't abandon you. You can come and pour your heart out to me anytime. There is nothing you can say or do that could ever make me stop loving you. If you don't feel like you can get through another week without your family, let's just take it day by day. Lean on me and if necessary we will very simply live one minute at a time. Everything is possible when you know you're loved and understood. Right?"* Compose something like that, that fits *your* circumstances and care for yourself as if you were your only child. Perhaps you could also do the Butterfly Hug as described in Chapter 16, as you reassure and love your fragile, lonely inner child.

In the same vein author Jack Kornfield, says: *"I used to think that to become free you had to practice like a samurai warrior, but now I understand that you have to practice like a devoted mother of a newborn child. It takes the same energy but has a completely different quality. It's compassion and presence rather than having to defeat the enemy in battle."*

Can you find moments when you stop warring in your mind with the JW 'religion' or even with yourself and turn to simply offering yourself some loving attention? Can you give up the struggle against the past and perhaps against yourself, come into the present moment and simply accept yourself just as you are? It's simple but not always easy. It is, however, one of the best ways to truly come home to yourself and improve the quality of your life.

When we are exiting a controlling, judgmental, unforgiving, punitive religious group our capacity for self-love and self-acceptance has been damaged. It is now up to you to repair this impaired ability to love yourself. It takes work. It takes persistence. It takes stopping the thoughts when you catch yourself thinking unloving things about yourself and replacing them with kind, warm, gentle thoughts of unconditional self-acceptance.

This is not a narcissistic or self-absorbed activity. It is an act of empathy and compassion. Once you have practiced and relearned how to give yourself unconditional acceptance you will not waste any more time preoccupied with yourself. Self-acceptance will simply become the inner holding environment from which you automatically flow with life.

Two thousand years ago Gautama Buddha said *"You, yourself, as much as anybody in the entire universe, deserve your love and affection."* Mark Twain said, *"The worst loneliness is to not be comfortable with yourself."* In spite of thousands of years of awareness of the vital need to accept and love ourselves, it is not always the first thing we think of doing, but do it we must! Thoreau said, *"It is what a man thinks of himself that really determines his fate."*

Perhaps as a child we never saw anyone look at us with eyes full of love. Perhaps no one ever told us how lovable we were (and are). If you were not blessed with the circumstances that conferred upon you this inner knowing, then it is up to you to do so for yourself. And, it bears repeating, you do not have to be perfect to be lovable.

Sometimes there seems to be an inner taboo, an inner aversion to loving ourselves. Carl Jung warned of this saying, *"The most terrifying thing is to accept oneself completely."* You must fight against the terror, taboo or aversion to loving yourself. Dr. Kristin Neff, author of Self-Compassion, says, *"I found in my research that the biggest reason people aren't more self-compassionate is that they are afraid they'll become self-indulgent. They believe self-criticism is what keeps them in line. Most people have gotten it wrong because our culture says being hard on yourself is the way to be."*

You've had the authoritarian Watchtower organization hovering over you with its rules, implied threats, warnings, and exhortations – trying to keep you in line. You will not become self-indulgent and wicked if you discontinue this unkind and unjust treatment and replace it with empathy and compassion. Unconditional self-acceptance will not happen overnight but with gentle, persistent awareness and loving attention you can finally give yourself the gift of unconditional acceptance.

Learning the approach to life called 'Mindfulness' is one method that can help you reclaim the presence required to love yourself. If you are depressed it is imperative that you relearn to love and accept yourself. Self-acceptance frees you up to experience joy. Joy is a healing emotion and one you deserve to experience.

Remember this self-love and acceptance is the key to all healing and creativity and only you can give this to yourself. It is not self-indulgent. It is not narcissistic. Your capacity to accept yourself has been damaged during your time spent in the JW cult and you must take on the task of repairing that damage. Once repaired it will just become the quiet underpinning of your identity. You will not even have to think about it, it will just be a permanent given of your life.

True narcissists are invariably people who on a deep level are full of self-hate and self-contempt usually due to early childhood neglect or abuse. Self-hate keeps such a person terribly preoccupied with getting the attention, recognition, approval and acclaim that might finally prove to themselves that they are lovable and worthy. True self-acceptance and self-love free us to live without that kind of self-absorption.

If you notice yourself thinking a self-critical, self-judgmental thought - stop it immediately and shift to a loving approach such as: "*I didn't perform well on that task. I could berate myself for the poor performance, and I have a choice. I choose to consider how I would perform differently in the future, rather than criticize myself for how I performed now. I deeply love and accept myself with all of my mistakes, limitations and problems. I do not have to be perfect in order to love and accept myself.*"

You don't pretend that you don't make mistakes or have occasional poor performances. Acknowledge them. If you can correct them, do. If you need to apologize or make amends, do. Consider how you would do things differently in the future. Give yourself credit for the effort and move on with what you have learned from the experience. Dwelling on self-criticism is totally counterproductive as it will only guarantee more of the same behavior (that you are criticizing) in the future.

"*Self-acceptance is my refusal to be in an adversarial relationship to myself.*"
Nathaniel Brand

Tell yourself the truth about an unsatisfactory situation, remark, performance, and then reframe it, as Carl Rogers did above, by seeing it as an enriching learning experience, as evidence of your unique set of crazy quirks. You have a choice as to whether you judge, blame and harshly criticize yourself. I love the words of Joseph Campbell, "*The privilege of a lifetime is being who you are.*" Be who you are and love your imperfect self just as you are. Isn't that ultimately, the deepest reason why we choose to leave the Jehovah's Witness cult - to be fully who we are?

You *could* find reasons to criticize yourself, *and you have a choice.* Choose self-acceptance and self-love. It will be such a refreshing change from what you learned and experienced in the JW cult. As a Witness it was clear that you could not speak truthfully about what you felt, what you experienced, what you wondered, how your thinking had evolved, what you really wanted, etc. To do so would be to violate an implicit group taboo and to put your membership in the group at risk. Wayne Muller, in his book "Legacy of the Heart" says, "*Self-acceptance is impossible if we cannot speak truthfully about ourselves. Without the truth we may learn to accept who we appear to be, but what we are accepting is a lie.*"

Now out of the restrictive, stifling milieu of the JW organization you can finally speak the truth about yourself – to yourself and others. In being able to be real and authentic you open the door to the gift of self-acceptance and self-love and vice versa.

If you would like to use affirmations to help deprogram yourself from old indoctrination and install new thoughts of self-love, self-esteem, self-forgiveness and well-being I recommend that you investigate the guided meditations of Louise Hay. One guided meditation that I particularly like on YouTube is entitled, "Louise Hay – Self-love Part 2." She also has dozens of others that you can try.

A Healing Technique Used in EFT Therapy:
(EFT stands for Emotional Freedom Technique)

EFT therapy was developed by Gary Craig and is based on Chinese principles of acupuncture and acupressure. (My favorite form of EFT is "*Faster EFT*" which is a derivative methodology developed by Robert G.

Smith.) In all forms of EFT instead of using needles in the acupuncture points, you tap or rub the points. There is a whole protocol for how, and in what order, etc. to tap on the various points. (See Resource Section on Alternative Therapies at the end of this book.) I offer the following simple one pressure point version for clients who need to do a little work on self-acceptance (and we all do).

Each of us has a sore or tender spot in the upper left quadrant of our chest. Just gently probe around the upper left side of your chest until you find your tender spot. Mine is about mid-point if you drew a diagonal line from the base of my neck to where my armpit begins.

Once you have identified where your 'sore spot' is you are going to gently rub it in a circular, clockwise motion while you repeat the following statement out loud or just in your mind:

> *"Even with all my problems and limitations, I deeply and com-pletely love, accept and forgive myself."*

Keep rubbing the spot and repeating the above statement to yourself for about a minute, more or less. Repeat the procedure a few times...as needed.

It is not necessary for you to consciously believe, at this moment, that you "*deeply love, accept and forgive yourself*". If you notice some resistance to that statement (and most of us do) you just repeat it anyway. You are trying to install the authentic state of positive regard for self and leave no room for the false state of negative regard for self. Your habituated mind is bound to resist a little at first. Just ignore the resistance to the statement and carry on. Since most of us have quite a load of self-hate in our unconscious, I would encourage you to do this daily for a while and then later on, use as needed.

As said earlier in this chapter self-acceptance and self-love are the key to all healing. This EFT technique helps us achieve that goal. It costs nothing,, cannot hurt you, can be done easily, so why not give it a try? By the way, the "sore spot" seems to continue to remain sore on everyone I've talked to. You are not looking to remove the tenderness from that spot. You are simply aiming to replace old, buried self-hatred with long overdue self-acceptance and rubbing the sore spot and saying the affirmation seems to help you do just that. I have added the word "*forgive*" to the EFT affirmation because I feel forgiveness facilitates love and acceptance (and vice versa). Over the years, there have been many things for which I have had to find a way to forgive myself. This EFT technique really helps accelerate the self-forgiveness process. Do try it.

I remember teaching this technique to a client who worked with an NGO and had just returned from a war-torn country. She had returned from her post with some PTS but as we worked together it became evident to me that she also had a buried childhood cache of unwarranted self-hate. I taught her this EFT technique and, in a rather patronizing tone, laced with a 'wink', she said she would give the little technique a try *if* she even managed to think of it during the week.

At the beginning of her next therapy session she enthusiastically reported in about her week saying it had been one of the best weeks she'd had since she returned from overseas. She described feeling more relaxed, less burdened, less anxious and less depressed. She added that she was more able to simply enjoy herself both while working and socializing. Then she suddenly paused and said, *"You don't think it's because of that silly, little rubbing thingy ... do you?"*

"So you did it? I asked.

"Yes, I actually did it a few times each day. That can't be what made me feel better...surely!?"

I smiled, pleased with what "silly little thingies" can sometimes accomplish. We have no way of knowing for sure if that EFT rubbing technique was what helped give the client some relief from her unconscious cache of self-hate and attendant anxiety and depression, but my guess is that it was a strong contributing factor. Why don't you give it a try – even if you, too, are a little skeptical about *"silly, little rubbing thingy"* techniques?

As you become accustomed to using the technique, you can then adapt it to specific feeling states or situations in your life. For example:

"Even with, <u>fill in the blank</u> I deeply and completely love, accept and forgive myself."

More Specific Examples:

"*Even with*, the panic I am feeling about being disfellowshipped and losing contact with my family, *I deeply and completely love, accept and forgive myself.*"

"*Even with*, the despair I am feeling about being shunned by my parents, *I deeply and completely love, accept and forgive myself.*"

"*Even with*, these feelings of loneliness and rejection, *I deeply and completely love, accept and forgive myself.*"

"*Even with*, the fact that I am told that I am an apostate and going to die at Jehovah's Battle of Armageddon, *I deeply and completely love, accept and forgive myself.*"

"*Even with*, the fact that my children are told to shun, fear and reject me, *I deeply and completely love, accept and forgive myself.*"

"*Even with*, the fact that I seem to be struggling with depression and some habitual feelings of self-hate and self-contempt, *I deeply and completely love, accept and forgive myself.*"

Some of the above statements may sound quite contradictory, but **say them anyway**! This is what your unconscious needs to hear, absorb and integrate.

CHAPTER 21

Self-Acceptance Linked to a Sense of Belonging

The thought of being cut off from loved ones awakens deep fears in every human being. Humans have a fundamental need to belong. Family is the main way that we achieve that sense of belonging. Family anchors us and is ideally a refuge from the storms of life. To have family torn away is traumatizing. However, when we lose loved ones there are alternative ways to get our belonging needs met – not necessarily the way we prefer to have them met, but met, nonetheless.

The most fundamental way to always have a sense of belonging is to unconditionally love accept yourself, as we talked about in the previous chapter. When you accept and love yourself you create a 'belonging' place within. You open your heart to yourself. You find a sense of belonging in your own heart - a place you can always turn to and find non-judgmental, open arms metaphorically waiting to welcome you.

If you lived as a Jehovah's Witness you probably had some sense of belonging within the organization and among the brothers and sisters - albeit a flawed, conditional belonging. I use the word "flawed" because if you wish to reconsider any of the beliefs or practices of the cult you are put on warning that you will lose your connection with, or belonging to, the group. Worse yet, they intimidate your loved ones into breaking connection with you too. All the sense of belonging experienced in the cult was/is conditional.

An organization that:

- limits the human connections you can make on this planet
- tells you that if you frequent people outside the group you are at risk of opening yourself to demonic influence
- places so many conditions on your belonging to the group
- has you suspicious about the motives of other humans and therefore limiting the connections you make
- requires you to live with many rules and on a strict, predetermined schedule
- requires you to limit outside activities, your information in-take, your reading materials, your level of education
- keeps you in a form of psychological confinement, isolation
- has members report to elders any 'un-witness-like' activities of fellow members

is an organization that has commandeered your life and has isolated you from others, the world, AND from yourself. Yes, your very self.

Time to Come Home to Yourself

It is time to finally come home and belong to yourself. One way to come home to yourself is of course, to leave the cult. An old Japanese proverb says, "*To know and not to act is not to know at all*". You know it is time to leave and to come home to yourself and if you are reading this book you have already done so or are taking steps to initiate the process. With the time you reclaim by leaving all the enforced busyness of the cult you can finally make your way back to yourself. How do you begin to make your way back to yourself and find a sense of belonging within yourself?

- take good physical care of yourself
- be emotionally kind to yourself
- listen to yourself
- trust your intuitions
- be supportive as you build a loving relationship with yourself
- allow yourself to sit, to be, to have moments with no agenda
- allow yourself to really understand, appreciate what you have been through and how courageous you have been

- promise yourself that you will not criticize or abandon yourself
- reassure yourself that the only one you can 'save' is you
- give yourself unconditional acceptance
- love yourself as if you were your only child
- find a sense of soft openness in your own loving heart

It is with such loving self-care that you can create a permanent sense of belonging within. No one can take an inner sense of belonging away from you. If you are being punished by the JW organization for daring to leave its ranks, punished by losing your fundamental connection and sense of belonging with loved ones who are still loyal JWs, then know you can always find a place of belonging in your own open and accepting heart.

Whether you are conscious of it or not, lack of love and acceptance for yourself ultimately means you have no inner sense of belonging. When we love our self, even when we lose everything and everyone, we know we still have a home in our heart. Teacher, Brene Brown in her book, "Daring Greatly" says, "...*our sense of belonging can never be greater than our level of self-acceptance.*

In the midst of the pain of being shunned you can experience the joy of having an inner refuge - that no one can take away. (See guided imagery in the next chapter.) Refuse to let the JW organization intimidate you with threats of taking away all belonging. They can take some, for a while, but they can never take away the true, ever-present home in your heart. Tara Brach says, "...*ultimately, our refuge is not outside ourselves, not somewhere in the future – it is always and already here.*"

The existential truth is, we will either leave or lose everyone that we love - sooner or later. It has been thus for everyone who has walked this planet. We all need a safe refuge within for those inevitable times when we lose loved ones and feel we have nowhere to turn. We need to know we can rest, recuperate, rejuvenate and always find total acceptance within. Mindfulness and loving-kindness meditation are techniques you can use to help access this unconditional belonging within. Once accessed, you are no longer dependent on external sources to fulfill your belonging needs.

"*I found myself praying: "May I love and accept myself just as I am.*" ~Tara Brach

CHAPTER 22

Creative Visualization as a Healing Resource

Visualization is a wonderful capacity of the mind. We all visualize future scenarios - especially when we worry. We often imagine all kinds of terrible possibilities and actually feel stressed and anxious due to our imaginings. We sometimes forget that we can harness this powerful capacity of the mind to visualize, and use this capacity to constructively and creatively help ourselves.

Creative visualization has received some bad press due to people who have co-opted and commercialized the technique with books claiming to show how to attract abundance or romance into your life. For now forget about the books that have exploited the technique. Psychologists, especially sports psychologists know visualizing works and teach it to their athlete clients all the time. Perhaps you have noticed elite athletes with their eyes closed before a performance or a competition visualizing every strategy or move they want to make. It is like an extra physical practice session because the body/mind cannot tell the difference between a real experience and a well-imagined one.

To demonstrate the power of creative visualization or guided imagery let's try **a little experiment.** As you read the following paragraph try to really sense (taste, smell, feel, hear, see) everything you read:

Imagine it's a scorching hot summer day. You've been outside working in the hot sun and your mouth is parched and dry. You decide to go inside and make yourself a delicious, ice cold lemonade drink, from scratch. You get a few lemons from the refrigerator and enjoying feeling their cool bumpy, yellow surface as you place them on the cutting board. As you take one beautiful juicy lemon and cut it with a sharp knife, you see glistening droplets of lemon juice squirt out from the lemon's yellow flesh. After slicing the lemon in two, you pick up one half and bring it up to your tongue and lick the wet, tart, acid, citrus flesh.

You should notice that you now have more saliva in your mouth than before you read the above paragraph. Just imagining the lemon and its spurting, tangy juices invariably produces the biological response of producing extra saliva in your mouth in anticipation of having to digest the lemon juices. *But you did not have an actual lemon, you were just visualizing that you did.* That is the power of creative visualization. Visualizing or imagining can produce actual biological responses because, again, our body/mind cannot tell the difference between a real experience and a really well-imagined one. Let's examine how we can harness this amazing mind/body response to make ourselves feel better as we work to heal from cult-control abuse.

Creative visualization can be used to vividly imagine scenarios or experiences that create biological responses that foster relaxation and well-being. There are a variety of resources you can purchase or view online designed to help you to relax and release stress using creative visualization or guided imagery. I love the ones that include actual sounds of nature as you follow along with the visualization (e.g. rain in a forest, waves lapping on the shore, a babbling brook, bird songs, etc.). These are great tools to use for managing stress – for example, if you are currently dealing with the stress of being shunned. Let's use some creative imagining right here to help release emotional toxins accumulated from being in a repressive cult.

A Guided Visualization:

Each day when you have a shower try to end the shower by gently changing the flow of water from warm to cool – a comfortable cool, not a shocking cool. I like to think of it as Earth cool. *Then, shut your eyes and as you stand there imagine (as vividly as possible) that you are in a beautiful, private spot in nature standing under a gentle, pure, cleansing waterfall. The air temperature is warm and beautiful rays of sunlight gently caress your skin. Give yourself permission to enjoy the earth-cool water flowing over every part of your body, restoring you, soothing you, healing you.......*

Now, further imagine that the magical waters are able to flow right through your skin, softly entering your body and gently flowing through every cell of your body. It's a lovely feeling. Know that as these healing waters flow softly through every tissue and structure of your body, they are taking away all the old unwanted beliefs, all the unreasonable expectations, all the woundedness stored in your body from your time in the JW cult. The cool, healing waters are washing all the hurtful holdings from your body, down into the pool of water below the waterfall... Just let it all go. Let all the indoctrination, all the hurt and all the stress be washed away... Take all the time you need to experience this as vividly as you can... Let the healing waters wash all the cult toxins and any resulting pain away into the outflow of waters in the pool below... Let any open, festering wounds you still harbor be closed and completely healed by the life-giving waters.............. Take all the time you need to accomplish this...

Notice and enjoy how much lighter you feel without the weight of all the old, toxic JW doctrines and expectations imbedded in the tissues of your body/mind.....

When you are ready, open your eyes and bring your awareness back to the here and now. Take a moment to get your bearings. (You can adapt the above visualization to a bath if you prefer. You may need to read the above visualization a few times so that you can easily bring it to mind in the shower!)

I live in a beautiful spot between a mountain and a river. There are several fresh mountain streams that make their way down the mountain to the river at its base. Whenever I am privileged to sit beside one, I creatively imagine that the flow of water is washing through my body and flushing away anything I have taken on that is not mine – anything that it would be healthy for me to release. I don't even have to know precisely what is being washed away. I just trust that what is not mine, what is toxic, what I don't need, what is unhealthy will be washed away by the flow of water. I allow myself to enjoy vividly imagining this for a few minutes. At the very least, this visualization is an extremely relaxing and stress-reducing exercise...and I have to admit I enjoy returning to my regular activities feeling every cell of my body has been washed clean of unwanted debris, whether physical, psychological, emotional or spiritual. You, too, can create your own spontaneous, creative visualization sessions just like this, as you enjoy moments in nature.

Here is **another guided visualization** I often used with clients who had abusive childhoods or who were experiencing difficult, painful emotions – for whatever reason. Read through it a couple of times to get familiar with it. When you want to actually do the guided visualization for yourself, simply read small portions of it at a time, then closing your eyes and imagining the portion of the guided visualization that you just read. Alternately, have someone you feel very comfortable with read it to you or record it with your own voice and replay whenever it suits you.

Take a moment to make sure you are sitting comfortably and when you are ready close your eyes. You are going to use your imagination to create the most beautiful, safe, comfortable, healing space for yourself. Decide if you want your healing space to be indoors or outdoors....... You are making a special, imaginary spot for yourself that is beautiful, peaceful, safe and healing ... and only yours. Take a few moments and create it just as you would like it to be..... (If you are creating an outdoor scene, make it the season and the time of day you most enjoy. Make this space a private place where you will not be disturbed and where you feel totally comfortable and safe. Be relaxed about creating this space, it does not have to be perfect or complete. You can always add or subtract elements in future visits back to this healing space.) *Once you have created this beautiful, safe, healing space in your imagination, visualize that you are finding a place to sit within the space and just soak up the beauty and the peace available to you there for a moment or two................*

As you sit there, you become aware that there is a gentle, non-threatening, benevolent presence in the space with you. (This presence could be an imaginary person, a beloved animal presence, a shimmer or ray of light, a beautiful cloud, any imaginary representation of a totally benevolent, loving presence that you want) You are amazed at how comfortable you feel with this gentle presence. In fact, you sense that somehow the presence knows you – has always known you, and loves you as a parent or grandparent would. There is no need to talk. You are able to communicate with each other without any sounds...............

What this presence is communicating to you is that it knows everything about you – all the good, all the special, all the adorable, all the not so adorable, all the not so good – and it brings absolutely no judgment to you. This gentle, benevolent presence completely understands everything you have been through and appreciates how hard you have struggled to survive some of the events of your life. You really sense the unconditional acceptance that this presence has for you. Remember, it has seen it all – the amazing things you have accomplished and also the less admirable moments of dishonesty, selfishness, insensitivity, and still, it does not judge you or stop loving you. This presence completely understands what it is to be a vulnerable human and it loves every part of you unconditionally no matter what has occurred in your past. You are amazed how totally relaxed you become when you realize there is no judgment, there are no conditions – there is just pure non-interfering and non-abandoning, loving presence. Soak up the unconditional love, the complete acceptance and the profound sense of understanding this presence offers you. Take all the time you need to complete this experience for yourself...............

When you are ready, say goodbye to this loving presence – just for now – knowing that you can return to this healing place and reconnect at any time. You know how to meet up with this presence now. As the presence leaves, without words it reassures you that it is always available to spend time with you and it hopes you will remember how loved and valued you are, even when you are not in each other's company...............

Open your eyes and gently bring your awareness back to the actual here and now. Sit for a moment where you are, and get your bearings back in the present moment. Notice how healing it is to feel completely and totally understood and accepted. Notice that this is a gift you have just given yourself using your faculty of creative imagination.

You do not have to depend on rare and often unreliable external resources to receive unconditional love and acceptance. **You can give yourself what you need when you need it.** Promise yourself that you will revisit your newly-created, safe place and this loving, healing presence often.

CHAPTER 23

Acting As If

Remembering what we learned from our imaginary lemon experiment in the last chapter - that the body/mind cannot tell the difference between a real experience and a well-imagined experience - let's explore some other ways we can apply this capacity of imagination to create a feeling of well-being during our recovery from being in a destructive cult.

As mentioned earlier we often experience physical effects such as butterflies in the stomach, sweaty palms, shallow breathing, rapid heartbeat, etc., from worrying, anticipating or imagining a worst possible scenario. Worry and anticipation happen in our imagination and we usually imagine that negative things will happen and the body/mind produces the corresponding physiological response, even though what we imagine is probably false and usually never happens. We can help ourselves by challenging our worry thoughts, asking *"Is that really true?" "Do I know for sure that these things will happen or am I just imagining the worst again?"* To stop the unwanted physiological responses stop the embellished, dread-full thinking, otherwise known as worry.

But what about using our imagination to produce a positive physiological response? I once saw a video of an interview of the Welsh stage and screen actor of the fifties and sixties, Richard Burton. It was well known that Burton was an alcoholic and frequently suffered from severe bouts of depression. The interviewer noted that Burton seemed to finally have conquered many of his psychological 'demons', was doing well, and asked him what accounted for the dramatic change. Burton's response went something like this: "*Well, in the midst of my last depressive episode, it occurred to me that I am an actor and it is said I'm a good one. So I thought, if I am such a good actor, why don't I just act as if I feel happy? Why don't I just act as if I expect life to be good and act as if I'm happy? And so I did. I just acted as if I felt great and went about my life. After a certain period of acting as if I was happy, I began to notice I really didn't have to act anymore. It seemed that by pretending I was happy, I eventually turned into someone who really was!*" (Paraphrased from memory.)

Burton acted as if he was happy and his body/mind could not tell the difference between a real experience of being happy and a well-acted (or imagined) experience of being happy. Since his body/mind was tricked into believing he was happy, one of the probable physiological responses was a re-wiring of the neural circuitry in his brain and soon he was able to stop acting and just be the satisfied, happy person he was meant to be.

Many refer to this strategy as, "*Fake it, til' you make it.*" Some clichés, like "*fake it til' you make it*" become popular because there is a strong element of truth in them. The idea is to fake feeling okay in spite of what has happened to you and after a while the feeling okay will become your default position. It's as if your internal systems say, "*Oh...it seems we're okay now. So let's produce the chemicals, hormones and neurological connections that go with the feeling of 'okayness' or happiness.*"

You can apply this 'acting as if' technique in many ways. You don't have to only pretend you are 'happy'. Maybe you want to *pretend* or *act as if* you are feeling positive instead of negative. Perhaps you want to pretend life is good and all will work out in the best possible way, even though you don't actually quite believe that yet. Perhaps you want to act as if you are confident, out-going, ready for any challenge, even though you aren't yet.

This is something you do in your head. It's private. There is no risk of public failure or humiliation. It costs nothing. You are going to live through the next few months anyway, why not live through them pretending you are feeling upbeat instead of actually feeling downtrodden?

Yes, I hear those of you saying, "*But it would not be the truth of how I feel! I would be living a lie. It wouldn't be authentic!*" That's right, but as the saying goes, sometimes desperate times call for desperate measures. Sometimes we have to be playful, creative and imaginative to facilitate our own healing. When children play 'pretend' to try out different personas and imagine themselves doing the things adults (or super-heroes) do, parents don't stop them saying, *"But that's a lie, sweetheart! You aren't really a superhero (ballerina, race car driver, fireman, etc.) Please darling, stop pretending and be authentic!"* No, parents understand that imaginary, pretend play is the way little human beings practice and learn different ways of being in the world. If a partner or friend questions you about your new attitude or approach, tell the truth. Don't lie to others if they need to know what you are doing. Let them know you are 'acting as if' and why. You could think of the technique as inauthentic, and you have a choice! I prefer to think of it as a creative strategy to experiment with a different approach to living before we have actually incorporated the approach into our life.

Another way to use this technique is to think of someone who has the approach to life that you would like to have. Then simply act as if you are moving through your life exhibiting the qualities and behaviors of that person. (It could be a person you know, or one you have admired from a distance, a character from a novel, whomever.) Pretend, imagine, act as if you have the attitude, perspective and qualities of the person you admire and notice the boost of energy, or confidence, or well-being you experience. Your body chemistry follows your thoughts, especially your well-imagined ones. You will not have to do this forever, only for a period of time until your body/mind has adopted or incorporated these new perspectives and qualities.

There are far reaching effects to making a shift to a more positive approach to life. Donna Eden in her book, Energy Medicine says, *"Your immune system can go astray by modeling itself after your behavior. Some immune disorders are, in fact, exact analogies of a person's way to relating to the world."* (p.242) If this is the case, it can be damaging to relate to the world as a depressed person. It can cause your immune system to become depressed too. If you have not been able to make an attitude shift of your own yet, you can consider simply pretending you have made the shift and benefit from all the systemic changes a well-imagined and well-acted approach can produce!

For example, you can make a shift from feeling like:

- you've been a victim of the Watchtower Society, *to acting as if* you are a survivor of JW.org and now thriving in spite of their abuse
- you're resentful and bitter about all you lost being a JW, *to acting as if* you have come to terms with your past in the JW ranks and are ready to move on
- you're mortally wounded by being shunned by your family, *to acting as if* you know that in spite of the pain of shunning, you can survive and must get on with life
- you're worthless and no good, *to acting as if* you know you matter, acting as if you absolutely know you have value and worth
- you'll never make up for all the time you lost as a member of the Jehovah's Witness cult, *to acting as if* you know you can apply yourself now and make a good life for yourself, regardless of the time stolen from you
- you have no confidence in your abilities, *to acting as if* you are confident and self-assured and that you can succeed with your projects
- you always see the glass as half empty, *to acting as if* you are now a person who sees the glass as half full

You get the idea. Making this imaginary shift helps change our internal images about our self, our expectations of our self, our perspective, our intentions, and of course, our confidence level. Since the beliefs and images we hold about our self have a huge impact on how we feel and behave, and therefore, on what happens to us, it makes sense to try this technique of "acting as if" we already possess the attitude or approach to life that we want and benefit from the resulting positive impact on our life. Then we abort the possibility of self-fulfilling prophecies based on negative feelings about our self, and open the possibility of self-fulfilling prophecies based on upbeat, confident feelings about our self.

At the very least acting as if you already have the qualities you want will give you some relief -- a little respite from negativity, doubt and depression. Even if you cannot sustain 'the act' all day long, doing it for a couple of hours a day is bound to make a shift in your physiological responses and help you feel better on many levels.

So, let's play pretend! The only thing we have to lose are some negative feelings about our self and our life. Here are some wonderful quotations from people far wiser than I, who support the idea of using your creative imagination to better your life:

> *"Imagine for yourself a character, a model personality, whose example you determine to follow, in private as well as in public."* Epictetus

> *"We are what we pretend to be, so we must be careful about what we pretend to be."* Kurt Vonnegut

> *"We do not need magic to change the world, we carry all the power we need inside ourselves already: we have the power to imagine better."* J.K. Rowling

> *"Live out of your imagination, not your history."* Stephen R. Covey

> *"Imagination, imagination, imagination! It converts to actual. It sustains, it alters, it redeems!"* Saul Bellow

> *"To bring anything into your life, imagine that it's already there."* Richard Bach

> *"All of imagination – everything that we think, we feel, we sense – comes through the human brain. And once we create new patterns in this brain, once we shape the brain in a new way, it never returns to its original shape."* Jay S. Walker

Use your imagination to *act as if* you feel the way you would like to feel and alter your brain's neural circuitry to your benefit! Act as if you feel positive about your prospects and your life, and enjoy the physiological benefits that accompany your new way of thinking about yourself.

CHAPTER 24

Take Time Before Embracing Another Religious Group

If you are contemplating leaving a cult or have just left one you are in a state of emergence and for a while in a state of emergency. Yes, *emergence*, arrival, unveiling, opening, new birth, etc. are almost always preceded by a sense of *emergency*. Many of the things you believed, many of the patterns of your life, many of the people you relied upon and loved, are going or are gone. You have departed a central, organizing component of your life. It is, for the psyche, a kind of death and therefore, a definite emergency. After a death, as already said, you will find yourself in a period of mourning. However, after the emergency of the death of old patterns, after the necessary period of mourning, you will eventually enter a period of re-stabilization and *re-emergence*. You were merged with a cult and you have emerged out of it. Wiggling your way out can leave you with a variety of injuries and you now need to heal the bumps, bruises, tears, violations and indignities. All of this takes time. Letting go and then regaining your balance as you re-emerge takes time because it is a process not an event. You honor your process when you allow the needed time for the situation to shift from one of **emergency to emergence**.

While at first you may feel like you are in free-fall, not finding anything familiar to hold on to, remember it is just a feeling and it will pass. Learn to simply allow the feelings and allow the emergency state and adjustment period to take its course without rushing to fix it. Just as your body knows how to heal itself after a serious surgery, so too your psyche knows how to heal the psychological and spiritual surgery (and emergency) of leaving your former beliefs and practices. Just as you must allow time and create the conditions that foster physical healing after actual surgery, so too for psychological and spiritual healing and emergence.

It is wise not to allow temporary discomfort or fear (emergency) to propel you into latching on immediately to another belief system with which you hope to assuage your angst. Take time to discover who you are without the illusory protection of another idealized parent substitute. It really is best not to immediately turn to another rescuer entity because you need time to allow your true self to emerge. You need time to discover what you value, what really matters to you, who you are on your own without any crutch. Give yourself time to experience all the losses involved in leaving one belief system and to grieve those losses before you muddy the fresh internal waters with new beliefs, more parental substitutes and more external expectations.

If you rush into the quick fix of another belief system or faith community you will abort your grieving process and it will then linger around in your body/mind quietly causing problems. Just as it pre-empts emotional healing to rebound into another love relationship after a split with a partner or lover, it pre-empts spiritual healing to rebound into another relationship with a belief system. You left the cult to reclaim your right to independence, your right to think for yourself. So why rush into immediately relinquishing this hard-fought-for personal autonomy? Give yourself time to heal and regain your footing as your true self before you embark down another path defined by anyone or anything else.

Personally, after I faded out of the cult I had no inclination whatsoever to attach myself to another religious or spiritual ideology. As far as man-made religious movements or faith communities were concerned I was totally risk averse. Years later as I read about Eastern philosophies such as Buddhism, Taoism and Advaita I was amazed at what sophisticated psychologies they were. (Eckhart Tolle's writings, for example, are almost identical to Advaita which are very simple, basic, humane, non-dual, non-denominational and consciousness-based.) None of the Eastern philosophies that intrigue me require faith in or worship of a god, but rather are treatises on how to walk through life consciously, simply, skillfully and compassionately. They are about ways of being, not ways of worshipping. In recent years both my husband and myself have tried to live our life following these presence-based, non-religious, modest, millennial years-old principles, embraced from various sources. Of course, I'm sure you will find *your* particular way to understand and live *your* life now that you are free to explore and *decide for yourself.*

Let's think again about how we can compare our break with the Watchtower Society to a symbolic surgery. Imagine the amputation of a diseased leg. After the amputation of a leg would doctors agree with a patient's demand to immediately apply a prosthetic leg? No, they would inform the amputee that they must allow time for the incision to heal and for all the internal structures (bone, muscle, cartilage, ligaments, nerves, etc.) to heal too. They would tell the patient that they need to become familiar with their new body as it is, without a support appendage and mourn the loss of the limb. While the amputee might firmly believe they need to feel supported by a solid leg substitute immediately, it is not in the best interests of their healing to rush in to fit and apply a prosthetic leg. In fact, without allowing the wound to properly heal, the fit would not be right. So too if we rush to get religious support (a kind of prosthetic) right away – our symbolic amputation's internal structures will not yet be healed, the immense loss will not be fully mourned, and the fit of the new religious 'prosthetic', or support, might not be right.

Once you feel you have debriefed yourself from the trauma of leaving your religious group, have grieved the losses, have become reconnected with your true self and your values, have made up for gaps in your adult development, then there will be plenty of time to exercise your hard-won freedom and make mature, adult, grounded decisions about what you believe and how you choose to express those beliefs.

Whatever you do, give yourself permission to enjoy your new free life, doing all the little things you have always wanted to do but couldn't because of all the restrictions imposed by a religious belief system. You are free! You have reclaimed time and space and now the only permission you need to explore, discover, choose and experience, is your own. Of course, being free you also have the choice to entirely ignore my suggestions about whether or not to espouse another religion or devotional community immediately.

When you have a moment, check out the inspiring poetry of Mary Oliver, especially her poem entitled *"The Journey"* where she talks about leaving the controlling external voices behind, to finally listen to the only voice that matters ...your own...and to save the only life you can possibly save...your own. Look for the poem *"The Journey"* in her book, Dream Work (1994), and on the internet.

Listen, as well, to the wise counsel of a husband and wife team of Gestalt therapists:

"One of the difficulties in moving out of the familiar is the temptation to close off the full drama of change before it ripens. The sense of being bereft of all that is familiar is a vacuum which threatens to suck up everything within its reach. What is hard to appreciate, when terror shapes a catastrophic gap, is that this blankness can be a Fertile Void. The Fertile Void is the existential metaphor for giving up the familiar supports of the present and trusting the momentum of life to produce new opportunities and vistas. The acrobat who swings from one trapeze to the next knows just when he must let go. He gauges his release exquisitely and for a moment he has nothing going for him but his own momentum. Our hearts follow his arc and we love him for risking the unsupported moment."

Erving & Miriam Polster

Once out of the Watchtower organization will you be willing to *"risk the unsupported moment"*?

CHAPTER 25

Governing Body Terrorizes
Its Own Members

S hunning is not only a terrible punishment for those who are shunned, it is also an unthinkable imposition for those required to do the shunning. It is unconscionable for the governing body to expect members of a family to be the symbolic executioners of their own loved ones! The rank and file of the Watchtower organization are told, "*Jehovah is watching us to see whether we will abide by his command not to have contact with anyone who is disfellowshipped.*" (Watchtower of April 15, 2012, p. 12)

There lies an implicit threat in that above statement from the Watchtower, that if members of the cult have contact with a disfellowshipped person, Jehovah is watching, Jehovah will remember, and if they do not abide by his command he may destroy them at Armageddon. With such insinuated threats of death at the always soon-to-arrive-Battle-of-Armageddon, the governing body of Jehovah's Witnesses is actually terrorizing and menacing its own members.

Most rank and file JW's are decent, good-hearted people. It should cut to the bone to be required to treat their loved one as dead, to be required to reject their loved one's companionship in order to prove their loyalty to Jehovah and the JW organization. It's as incomprehensible as their obedience to the requirement that parents prove their loyalty to Jehovah and JW.ORG by refusing life-saving blood treatments for a sick child. We could well expect the internal conflict and despair these inhumane requirements cause JW members, to be unbearable, *but* the calculated indoctrination that circumvents their critical thinking skills also seems to interfere with their normal human love and compassion. Surely only a sociopathic climate in an organization's upper echelons could dare to go so far as to force the rupture of normal, loving, familial bonds.

The governing body claims their authority to make such cavalier orders comes from Jehovah God. But what kind of a god would require these inhumane behaviors of his followers? No all-loving, compassionate god would. Only a god who is more a projected representation of human pathology and extremism than an actual loving heavenly Father would treat his loyal believers in such a way. These punishments and requirements are contrivances of a governing body afraid to lose power over its domain, using every tactic at its disposal, without conscience, to retain control over the lives of its indentured servants. How contemptible and cunning to threaten, intimidate and terrorize its members and to then claim the harsh requirements actually come from God Almighty.

We must have compassion for our friends and family still caught in the JW cult who are brainwashed, intimidated and pressured to go against their own innate goodness and cut off all association with their loved ones. While rank and file JWs have to accept responsibility for their choices and actions, they *are* suffering from the merciless tactics of the JW governing body just as we are. They are in an awful catch-22 situation imposed upon them by their leadership. Choosing to blame or resent our loved ones for the choices they are duped and forced to make only burrows a hole deeper into our own hurting heart. We must let go of blame and think of their brainwashed plight with empathy. We do this as much for ourselves as for them.

If you as an ex-JW are being shunned, there is no way to not experience the pain of it. It is designed by the perpetrators to be painful, and it is. I so wish I had a magic formula or a magic wand to offer you in order to eliminate the pain of such ruptures. All I can do is assure you that with time the wound becomes less raw, stops actively gaping and bleeding, and is no longer as crippling as it is in the beginning. This horrible treatment requires that we give ourselves a lot of compassionate self-care.

It is a comfort to know that there are determined ex-JWs working through the judicial systems in various countries to have shunning declared the criminal violation of human rights that it is. Wouldn't it be satisfying to see governments step in to defend individuals and families from the barbaric tactics of this destructive cult?

There are more and more former Jehovah's Witnesses who are publically exposing JW.ORG's unwarranted sanctions on its followers for the simple act of wanting to end their membership in their organization. If you have the strength and inclination to add your voice to the thousands who are now rising up in protest, please find a way to do so.

We are beginning to see evidence that the Watchtower organization is being profoundly affected by all the public exposure, denouncements, protests, lawsuits and verdicts against their policies and practices. With the advent of the internet and social media they are unable to keep their medieval policies, practices and abuses secret any longer. They are now scrambling to re-organize and re-brand themselves. JW.ORG is frantically into damage control. They are also trying to relax (dumb down?) some of their superficial, discretionary practices while at the same time doing all they can to tighten their grip on the membership who are still 'true believers'. Such desperate measures do not portend well for the future JW.ORG.

As well, with all the internal upheaval, public pressure, soaring legal costs and public exposure, we just never know what could happen down the road. Let's hold the hope that the JW organization will soon collapse upon its vapid, empty self. If and when that happens, your family will be free to love and embrace you again. Do not give up hope that your loved ones will one day see the light and stop feeling they have to obey the governing body's commands. It is comforting once in a while to spend a moment to fantasize about thousands of long-overdue family reunions. However, since we can't count on that fantasy coming true, it is best that we concentrate our efforts on *our* personal healing journey, *our* individual march to freedom, and when appropriate, *our* public denunciation of this misbegotten, heartless pseudo-religion.

"...the greatest threat and greatest cause of anxiety ... near the end of the twentieth century is not castration but ostracism, the terrible fate of being exiled by one's group. Many a contemporary man castrates himself or permits himself to be castrated because of fear of being exiled if he doesn't. He renounces his power and conforms under the great threat and peril of ostracism." ~Rollo May

CHAPTER 26

Ruptured Families –
Some Context

Sometimes a little context can help give some fresh perspective. We tend to think, in the midst of our pain that only ex-Jehovah's Witnesses are torn away so brutally from their families, but in fact separation from family of origin has been endured by humans through the centuries. Humans have, in both past and present, experienced rupture and estrangement from their families in the some of the following ways:

- slavery
- kidnapping
- military service
- immigration
- sexual orientation
- expulsion
- choice of career
- marriage partner
- plague
- genocide, pogroms
- changing religion
- political party
- impenetrable borders
- racism
- natural disaster

- criminal activity
- intractable arguments
- prison, internment
- mental illness
- poverty
- abandonment
- death
- philosophical differences

Even at the moment of birth we are expelled from our home in the womb and ripped from the umbilical cord. It seems that being severed from what we know (mother, home, homeland, family) is almost a prerequisite for human growth and development, and our entrance into the world is but a foreshadowing of more separations to come.

Is it perhaps an evolutionary imperative that in one way or another we have to lose our comfort zone, our familiar patterns, our home base, in order to grow up and assume our full responsibilities as an adult self? The pervasive nature of familial ruptures across the centuries and across cultures could certainly make one speculate in the affirmative.

The harsh reality of life on Earth is that sooner or later we will lose or leave everyone that we love. Some of these difficult familial splits may serve as preparation for the inevitable future losses that human life entails. A rather discouraging thought but we are here to deal with what is, to speak the truth about it, and hopefully gain a little perspective on our current circumstances.

While none of the above listed causes of family ruptures, demonstrating the extent to which family units have been torn asunder throughout the ages, attenuates the pain of *our* separation and *our* banishment from loved ones, it does demonstrate that in such ruptures and such estrangements we are not alone or unique.

Change and suffering are a part of the human experience. Is it so, perchance, because suffering is one of the surest paths to awakening to the truth of our existence? Suffering was, in large measure, the catalyst for awakening from the trance of being a Jehovah's Witness. Free of the pseudo-religion, and suffering anew because of their punishments, what are we now being called to awaken from or to? The suffering is an invitation into an existential awakening that each of us must assume on our own. The question is, can we rise above our particular circumstance of suffering and see the bigger picture? What opportunity lies buried in our particular suffering scenario? Therapist and writer Wayne Muller says, *"Beneath all the stories of our past, beneath our joys and sorrows, we have within us an essential nature that is whole and unbroken... If we can take nourishment from this inner strength and wisdom, we will find great peace and courage."*

For some, especially those who are still psychologically or spiritually asleep, pain is simply something that they want to stop as soon as possible. For others pain serves as a clarion call to pay attention, to finally stop and look at the bigger picture, to think more deeply about life, to determine in what measure they can open their heart and to discover the further levels of inner growth still possible.

I hope you can use the seemingly inevitable pain of separation and estrangement from loved ones to propel you to a higher level of openness, sensitivity, presence, consciousness, and action. **Try to take the view that the pain is not there to oppress you, but to awaken you,** if you are able to look beyond the immediacy of the actual suffering to the prompt hidden within it.

Suffering, it seems, is the universal, symbolic vehicle we must ride to arrive at the mysterious, ever-alluring destination called *Awakening.*

Contemplate the following thoughts on awakening or enlightenment:

"The journey is simply a reawakening to the knowledge of where you always were and what you always have been. It is a journey without distance to a goal that has never changed." Alan Watts

"An inner wholeness presses its still unfulfilled claims upon us." Emma Jung

"We know the immensities of space better than we know our own depths, where, even though we do not understand it, we can listen directly to the throb of creation." Carl Jung

"There is no way of telling people that they are all walking around shining like the sun." Thomas Merton

CHAPTER 27

How Do I Proceed From Here?

If you are suffering due to the punishment of shunning by your JW family and friends you have a choice: you can wallow in it and prolong the suffering, *or* you can ask yourself that Zen question: "*This being the case, how do I proceed from here?*"

If you asked that Zen question of me with regard to the painful experience of being shunned, I would reply:

- with head held high
- without denying the pain
- taking the time you need to mourn your losses
- slowly, tenderly
- with determination and courage
- with love, acceptance and compassion for yourself
- summoning all the self-esteem and self-worth, you can find
- with compassion for loved ones required to shun you
- with the knowledge that change is inevitable and anything can happen including perhaps a future reunion with your family
- with the knowledge that time heals all wounds, even these
- knowing your heart has an infinite capacity to love and though you may not always be in personal contact with your family of origin, you can add many new, rewarding, loving relationships to your life now

- knowing that life needs your contribution - needs you to go on in spite of the pain of being duped, deceived, disrespected and discarded
- knowing that millions before you have survived profound loss, estrangement and grief and you can too
- knowing there are many ex-JWs out there, also being shunned, who might be happy to make a connection with you
- knowing that you can allow this suffering experience to emotionally destroy you, *or* you can use it to awaken yourself to who you really are and to a brand-new perspective on reality

To that same Zen question "... *how do I proceed from here?*" Rainer Maria Rilke would answer:

"Be patient toward all that is unsolved in your heart ... and try to love the questions themselves ... And the point is, to live everything. Live the questions now. Perhaps you will then gradually, without noticing it, live along some distant day into the answers." (Letters to a Young Poet, p. 35)

To that same Zen question, Carl Jung would answer:

"The meaning of my existence is that life has addressed a question to me ... or conversely, I myself am a question." (Memories, Dreams, Reflections, p. 318)

So much of life is a magnificent mystery - so much remains curiously unresolved. As Jung suggests we may not find *the* answer or *the* meaning of it all because our life itself seems to be an unfolding, on-going question. How dare any man-made organization or quasi-religion pretend they have the answers for us all and threaten that we will lose our families and friends and die at God's Battle of Armageddon if we do not accept their answers!

When we walk away from all those bogus, man-made solutions of the JW cult (which may be all we have ever known) and are thereby made dead to those we love, we are left with our one and only life and the beautiful, exciting question it is. Rilke reframes the lack of answers to the ongoing mystery of life and to an opportunity to live the questions themselves - to even love the unresolved questions - and thereby to grow into the best, curious, evolving, free human we can be. And one day as we live with the unresolved questions (not demanding, like a child, to have the immediate gratification of packaged, patronizing answers) we may find that we have lived our way into an understanding of life that could only have evolved when we had the courage to live without the crutch of someone else's answers.

Existential-Humanist Doctor of Psychology, James Bugental sums it up beautifully: *"Our homeland is within, and there we are sovereign. Until we discover that ancient fact anew and uniquely for each of us as individuals, we are condemned to wander, seeking solace where it cannot be found, in the outer world."*

Given our circumstance we must proceed with our one and only life by seizing the opportunity, free from the cult, to discover the solace and power of our *inner sovereignty*. Our true self has been waiting for us to come home and honor all that we individually are and all we can be when a self-serving, manipulative, external force is no longer allowed to interfere with our life.

So, how will you proceed from here? Will you claim sovereignty over your life? Will you find yourself worshipping forever at the seductive, sometimes self-absorbed, altar of suffering? *Or* will you embrace the challenge of living the questions you encounter in the suffering and allow your allotted portion of suffering to be a guide leading you to a more awakened understanding of life? Suffering, for a while, after leaving JW.ORG seems to be a given. How you respond to that suffering is your sovereign choice.

CHAPTER 28

There Must Be a Pony Here Somewhere

Have you heard the old story about the ever-optimistic little boy who even when he encounters a room packed full of horse manure exclaims, *"With all this manure, there must be a pony in here somewhere!"* May each of us find a pony in the pile of manure inflicted upon us by the Watchtower organization in the form of their lies, indoctrination, shaming and shunning!

Teacher and author, Sharon Salzberg says: *"The key to our deepest happiness lies in changing our vision of where to find it."*

Perhaps, just perhaps, along with the pain, in the midst of the pain, even because of the pain, you will find something of value in this wretched, malodorous experience of being shunned:

- The value may be that the pain itself pulls you into the present moment and the peace it holds.
- The value may be that in the pain of aloneness you finally make a connection to your true self that you could never have made otherwise.
- The value may be the inner growth and maturity you claim at the other end of the worst part of the pain.
- The value may be the discovery of your innate resilience and psychological strength while living with all these losses, disappointments, insults and injuries.

- The value may be in the courage you find in knowing that you now can survive anything.
- The value may be in the discovery that your own heart is spacious enough and strong enough to hold the most difficult of losses.
- The value may be that no matter what a perverse organization does or threatens to do, they cannot disturb the love in your heart for yourself and your family - and even in the unconscionable, enforced absence of family you can still hold tightly to that love.
- The value may be the new family you create when you realize that, for now, you can no longer enjoy in person the love of your JW family of origin.
- The value may be in the permanent sense of home and belonging you create in your own heart.
- The value may be that you get to know yourself, as you could never have done as a clone in a cult.
- The value may be in the personal responsibility you learn to assume for your attitude in the face of whatever life throws at you.
- The value may be that you learn to live life as a compelling question, not murdering the mystery of it with pre-packaged answers from an outside source.

A new understanding of existence and a new, exciting life path can be found in the midst of the suffering you experience as a result of JW deception, injustice and shunning. Focus on all the learnings, all the gifts and the many wonderful possibilities contained within your hard-won freedom and not only on the suffering that comes with it. Find the new life (the pony) buried under the pile of manure (the aftermath, mayhem and rubble of being a JW). In that way the suffering will gradually lose its impact and your free, awakened life will truly begin.

Postscript

In her book of poetry *"Under the Waves"* Kaveri Patel has a beautiful poem entitled *"A New and Deeper Truth"*. In this poem Kaveri speaks about *"the old truth"* that has us fleeing for deliverance and relief as one would run from an arid desert toward a lush, green oasis. She describes *"the old truth"* as being full of *"toxic judgments"* that suck the life out of us. Sounds rather familiar, doesn't it?

Kaveri then encourages us once out of the desert of the old truth to simply sit and *"inhale the breeze of kindness"* as a *"new and deeper truth"* flows into us from the non-judgmental, non-demanding, welcoming waters at the long-sought oasis of the true self.

Now out of the desert of arid, life-choking doctrines and practices of the JW cult you are free to luxuriate, grow and find fulfillment in the oasis of a new and deeper truth – your own!

Recommended Reading

Books are listed alphabetically by author, although the title of the book appears first in the description. Books with asterisks are written specifically about JWs.

Healing Anxiety and Depression, 2004, Daniel G. Amen
Losing Faith in Faith, 2006, Dan Barker
Religion Explained, 2002, Pascal Boyer
The Other Side of Sadness, 2010, George A. Bonanno
Radical Acceptance, 2004, Tara Brach
True Refuge, 2013, Tara Brach
Calming Your Anxious Mind, 2006, Jeffrey Brantley
*Judgment Day Must Wait, 2013, Poul Bregninge
Daring Greatly, 2012, Brene Brown
The Healing Power of the Breath, 2012, Brown & Gerbarg
*No Room to Move, 2013, Alan Butters
*Captives of a Concept, 2005, Don Cameron
The Artist's Way, 2002, Julia Cameron
Living Beautifully With Uncertainty and Change, 2013, Pema Chodron
How to Meditate, 2013, Pema Chodron
Taking the Leap, 2010, Pema Chodron
When Things Fall Apart, 2000, Pema Chodron
The Places That Scare You: A Guide to Fearlessness in Difficult Times, 2002, Pema Chodron

Start Where You Are, 2001, Pema Chodron
The EFT Manual, 2011, Gary Craig
Finding Flow, 1997, Mihaly Csikszentmihalyi
Identity and the Life Cycle, 1994, Erik Erikson
Man's Search for Meaning, 2006, Viktor E. Frankl
In Search of Christian Freedom, 2007, Raymond Franz
Crisis of Conscience, 2004, Raymond Franz
Jehovah's Witnesses, 2001, Edmond C. Gruss
Free Will, 2012, Sam Harris
Waking Up: A Guide to Spirituality Without Religion, 2014, Sam Harris
Freedom of Mind, 2012, Steven Hassan
Combatting Cult Mind Control: 25th Anniversary Edition, 2015, Steven Hassan
Conscious Living: Finding Joy in the Real World, 2001, Gay Hendricks
Why Religion Is Immoral, 2015, Christopher Hitchens
The True Believer, 2002 (1951), Eric Hoffer
Hauntings – Dispelling the Ghosts Who Run Our Lives, 2013, James Hollis
What Matters Most, 2009, James Hollis
On This Journey We Call Our Life, 2002, James Hollis
Creating A Life, 2000, James Hollis
Swamplands of the Soul, 1996, James Hollis
The Grief Recovery Handbook, 2009, James & Friedman
Full Catastrophe Living, 2013, Jon Kabat-Zinn
Wherever You Go, There You Are, 2005, Jon Kabat-Zinn
Think Smarter: Critical Thinking, 2014, Michael Kallet
Who Would You Be Without Your Story?, 2008, Byron Katie
Loving What Is: Four Questions That Can Change Your Life, 2003, Byron Katie
The Ghosts from Mama's Club, 2012, Richard E. Kelly
Three Books: Body Rags, Mortal Acts, Mortal Words, the Past, 2002, Galway Kinnell
Recovery from Cults, 1995, Michael D. Langone
Out of the Cocoon, 2010, Brenda Lee
The Children Act, 2014, Ian McEwan
How Then, Shall We Live?, 1997, Wayne Muller
Legacy of the Heart: The Spiritual Advantages of a Painful Childhood, 1993, Wayne Muller
Self-Compassion, 2011, Kristin Neff
The Book of Awakening: Having the Life You Want by Being Present to the

Life You Have, 2000, Mark Nepo
Yoga for Anxiety, 2010, Mary Nurrie Stearns
Beauty: The Invisible Embrace, 2005, John O'Donohue
To Bless the Space Between Us, 2008, John O'Donohue
Dream Work, 1994, Mary Oliver
The Mindful Way Through Anxiety, 2011, Susan M. Orsillo, Lizabeth Roemer
Tapping In: A Step-By-Step Guide to Activating Your Healing Resources Through Bilateral Stimulation: 2008, Laurel Parnell
Under the Waves, Kaveri Patel, 2012
Coming Home to Who You Are, 2011, David Richo
The Five Things We Cannot Change ... and the Happiness We Find by Embracing Them, 2006, David Richo
How to Be An Adult: A Handbook on Psychological and Spiritual Integration. 2002, David Richo.
Letters to A Young Poet, 1986, Rainer Maria Rilke
8 Keys to Safe Trauma Recovery, 2009, Babette Rothschild
Compassion and Self-Hate, 1975, Theodore I. Rubin, M.D.
Loving-Kindness: The Revolutionary Art of Happiness, 2002, Sharon Salzberg
The Divided Mind, 2006, John E. Sarno, M.D.
The Mindbody Prescription, 1999, John E. Sarno, M.D.
The Instinct to Heal, 2004, David Servan-Schreiber
Getting Past Your Past, 2012, Francine Shapiro
Mindsight: The New Science of Personal Transformation, 2010, Daniel, J. Siegel
The Untethered Soul, 2007, Michael A. Singer
A New Earth: Awakening To Your Life's Purpose, 2008, Eckhart Tolle
The Power of Now, 2004, Eckhart Tolle
Yoga for Depression, 2003, Amy Weintraub
*Awakening of a Jehovah's Witness, 2002, Diane Wilson
The Spinoza Problem: A Novel, 2013, Irvin D. Yalom
Cracking the Cult Code for Therapists: What Victims of High-Control Groups Want Their Therapists to Know, to be published in 2017, Bonnie Zieman
*Fading Out of the JW Cult: A Memoir, 2016, Bonnie Zieman
The Challenge to Heal – After Leaving a High-Control Group, 2016, Bonnie Zieman

About the Author

After thirty years as one of Jehovah's Witnesses, Bonnie Zieman slowly faded her way out and finally obtained the higher education she had been denied as a member of this education-phobic cult. Using her university education and other extensive training to become a 'wicked' licensed psychother-  apist, she worked with clients in private practice for over twenty years. Bonnie has written several books related to recovery from high-control group abuses. Bonnie lives near Montreal, Canada with her husband Terry, also an ex-JW. They enjoy a life free from all the information, behavior, and mind control they were subjected to for so many years in this destructive cult. Their three adult children also enjoy fulfilling lives free of JW.ORG indoctrination and interference.

Bonnie Zieman's Latest Book
(to be released in 2017)

Index

Made in the USA
Columbia, SC
15 February 2020